The Essential Guide to the SAT

Written by:
Dawn Burnette
Stefan France
Terry Wilfong

Guest Writers:
Diane Darling
Erin Gard
Real experiences from the perspective of real students

Contributions by:
Joyce Suber

Version II 2008-2009

ISBN-13: 978-1-60352-593-0
ISBN-10: 1-60352-593-9

Table of Contents

Introduction.. 5

Chapter One
    Essential Facts.. 7

Chapter Two
    Test-Taking Tips... 9

Chapter Three
    Verbal Skills Review.. 11

Chapter Four
    Math Skills Review.. 47

Chapter Five
    Practice Test.. 109

Chapter Six
    Practice Test Answers (with explanations)... 143

Chapter Seven
    Additional Resources... 167

(Answer sheets for taking the Practice Test can be found at the back of the *Guide*.)

Introduction to The Essential Guide

Welcome to the world of *SAT* test prep. Like thousands of other high school students, you are probably both excited and anxious about all of the steps that will lead you to a college that is right for you. Among those steps is taking college entrance exams, so, perhaps you are wondering what you can do to make sure that you achieve your very best on these tests. Well, not to worry. Help is on the way!

Overview and Goals of the *SAT* Prep Program

Our materials are designed for students who want to increase their scoring potential or improve on previous scores on the *SAT* and for those who are seeking a refresher course in particular verbal, writing, and/or math skills.

Our program is designed to boost your confidence in taking college entrance exams by providing:

- vital information about the nature and construction of the *SAT* and about test registration;
- tips for mastering the art of taking standardized tests in general and the *SAT Reasoning Test*, specifically;
- formal instruction and tips for tackling test prep and taking the exam;
- help for increasing your reading vocabulary;
- the student perspective on issues related to college entrance testing;
- a fun way—in video game format—for reviewing material and practicing test-taking skills;
- a brief bibliography of other resources to aid you in preparing for the *SAT Reasoning Test*.

In fact, we believe that we offer you a unique approach to mastering the *SAT*. Our approach is tailored to students who are self-motivated — those who can and will work on their own in preparing for the *SAT*, but who are not interested in using the typical "big, fat book" of 200+ pages to do so.

Included with this guide is a fun, easy-to-use practice test in the form of an *SAT* test prep game called *Zero Hour Threat*. Created by I.D.E.A.S. at the Disney-MGM Studios, it is an interactive action game designed to increase standardized test scores as well as enhance general mathematics and vocabulary skills. With each correct answer, students move one step closer to decoding a virus that international criminals have set in place to infect the United States, banking systems. You will be able to work on enhancing your *SAT Reasoning Test* scores while having fun by playing a state-of-the-art video game. The *Zero Hour Threat* CD is not a stand-alone study program. It is designed for use in conjunction with the review materials, questions, and other tools provided in *The Essential Guide to the SAT*.

In addition to the CD game, you will find skill-building exercises, along with practice questions in each category of the *SAT Reasoning Test* and one 3 hour 45 minute practice test to provide you with a simulated experience in taking the actual *SAT*. For each of these, we will provide the opportunity for you to score your test by providing the correct answers and the rationale behind each of those responses.

Frequently Asked Questions and Student Concerns

Below is a list of some frequently asked questions and concerns raised by students regarding the *SAT Reasoning Test*.

- Why should I take the *SAT Reasoning Test*?
- What is the difference between the *SAT Reasoning Test* and the *SAT Subject Tests*?
- How do I register for *SAT* exams?
- What subjects are covered on the *SAT Reasoning Test*?
- How is the *SAT* scored?
- What tools may I or should I bring to the *SAT* test site on the day of the exam?
- What is the format of the exam?
- How can I prepare for the exam?
- Which method of preparation for college entrance testing is best?
- How long should I spend on each question?
- If I don't know the answer to some questions, should I guess?

Each of these questions will be addressed in the appropriate chapters of the *Guide*. You should read each chapter carefully and thoroughly in order to make the most of the material provided. You should also jot down any other questions that come to mind as you read and engage in the activities found in each chapter. If you find that you have additional questions or concerns, you may consult the guidance or college counselor at your school or visit the *College Board* website at www.collegeboard.com for further information about *SAT* tests.

Optimizing Your Use of *The Essential Guide to the SAT*

To get the most out of the *Guide*, we suggest that you follow the directions to the letter. You should plan to work with the written material a chapter at a time, setting aside time each day for studying the content and completing the exercises. On a daily basis, review the *SAT* vocabulary building material (provided in the verbal review section of the *Guide*), using the suggested strategies for increasing your reading comprehension and writing an effective essay. And you can, of course, play *Zero Hour Threat* as frequently as time permits. (Remember that getting into college depends largely on your academic performance and that success at school is a result of hard work in the classroom and completion of your homework and other assignments.)

We hope that you will find our approach exciting and rewarding. After utilizing this unique test preparation method that combines work and play, you should be on your way to increasing your *SAT* scoring power.

> Using *The Essential Guide to the SAT* will…
>
> 1) Boost your confidence
> 2) Increase your potential for high scores
> 3) Increase your vocabulary
> 4) Help you master the art of test-taking

Chapter One: Essential Facts

What is the SAT?

The *SAT* college entrance examinations, designed and developed by *The Educational Testing Service (ETS)* in Princeton, New Jersey and administered by *The College Board*, are taken by more than 2 million people annually. There are two categories of this examination program—the *SAT Reasoning Test* and the *SAT Subject Tests*.

SAT Reasoning Test

This exam assesses critical thinking abilities necessary for successful college level study. It is a 3 hour 45 minute test that utilizes verbal and mathematical questions to measure skill in essay writing, critical reading/sentence completion, and grammar/use of conventions, as well as mathematical reasoning.

The test begins with a writing section during which you are asked to demonstrate your ability to express yourself effectively by writing a brief, well-organized essay. This essay should reflect skill in stating and supporting a main idea and in utilizing proper sentence structure and diction. After completing your essay, you will be tested on the remaining skills—critical reading/comprehension/sentence completion; grammar/writing conventions; and mathematics — through 20- and 25-minute sections presented in random order.

Each section — writing, reading, and mathematics — can result in scores ranging from 200 to 800 for a total score ranging from 600 to 2400. (One of the 25-minute sections, called the "equating" or "variable," will not be scored or reflected in your total score. The questions in this section are used to analyze questions for use on future exams and do not count in scoring the exam.) Below is a chart that summarizes the contents of the *SAT Reasoning Test*:

> **Critical Reading** (200-800 points)
> (Multiple-choice responses to passage reading; sentence completion)
> Two 25-minute sections
> One 20-minute section
>
> **Mathematics** (200-800 points)
> (Multiple-choice and student-generated responses to numbers and operations, algebraic functions, geometry, probability, statistics, and data analysis)
> Two 25-minute sections
> One 20-minute section
>
> **Writing** (200-800 points)
> (Short essay measuring organization, development of main idea, sentence structure, and diction; multiple choice)
> One 25-minute section (essay)
> One 35-minute section (identifying errors; improving sentences and paragraphs)

SAT Subject Tests

These tests are designed to allow students the opportunity to demonstrate their knowledge in specific areas of study. Formerly called the *SAT II, Subject Tests* are offered in five categories—English, history/social studies, mathematics, science, and languages. Each *Subject Test* is a 1-hour multiple-choice examination, allowing students to take up to three tests on the same day. (For detailed information about the *SAT Subject Tests*, visit *www.collegeboard.com*.)

Who Should Take the *SAT Reasoning Test*?

As a college entrance examination, the *SAT Reasoning Test* is taken largely by high school juniors and seniors. Most American colleges and universities accept the *SAT*, along with a record of academic performance (the high school transcript), evidence of involvement in extra- and co-curricular activities, recommendations, essays, and other supportive documents, as a part of the application profile of potential students.

Since the *Reasoning Test* measures mathematics through the third year of college preparatory study, we recommend that students take their first *SAT Reasoning Test* no earlier than the spring of their junior year in high school, unless they are highly advanced in their academic work. The majority of colleges record their applicants' *SAT* scores using the highest score achieved in each area of the test. Therefore, students who achieve a high score in one or two areas but feel the need to improve on scores in other areas should feel free to take the exam again, prior to their college application deadlines.

How do I register for the SAT and what fees apply?

Test registration materials are available in your high school guidance or college counseling office. You will find test dates and registration deadlines posted in both of these locations as well.

You can also register online at *www.collegeboard.com*. There are many advantages to registering online, including the ability to confirm your registration, print your *SAT* test admission ticket, and receive or send your exam scores.

The fees for taking the *SAT Reasoning Test* and the *SAT Subject Tests* are outlined in the registration materials or may be found online at *www.collegeboard.com*. Since additional fees may apply under various circumstances, it is wise to read the registration material carefully.

You may be eligible for a fee waiver to offset the costs related to *SAT* tests. (This may also apply to college application fees at colleges that work in cooperation with the *SAT* Fee Waiver Service of *The College Board*.) Fee waiver information is available through your guidance or college counselor, and fee waiver cards can be procured only from the counselor, even for online registration. Home-schooled students must provide the local high school proof of eligibility for fee waivers. To use the card, you must register for the *SAT* exams according to regular posted deadlines.

Chapter Two: Test-Taking Tips

The next two chapters will focus on the review of skills related to the areas tested on the *SAT Reasoning Test*. Along with skill review, you will find tips and strategies for tackling specific types of questions. This chapter will center on general tips for taking standardized college entrance tests. While we cannot guarantee that these tips will work for every student, you should consider them as good advice for any test-taker.

Nora, a student who recently took the SAT, offers the following advice:

- **Dress in layers and bring a sweater or jacket.**
  Test sites use the cafeteria, auditorium, or other spaces that are large enough to hold all of the test-takers, but schools often turn off the heat or air conditioning on the weekends. It is difficult to concentrate when you are too hot or too cold.

- **Bring a watch.**
  Basic time management is up to you! The proctors tell you how much time you have for each section, when to start, when to stop, and when you have 5 minutes left. You should pay attention to how long you are taking on the questions and pace yourself during the test.

- **Skip hard questions or use your best guess.**
  You can usually narrow your choices down to two possible correct answers. That will give you a 50% chance of answering the question correctly. (We will cover guessing in more detail below.) Approaches to this strategy differ when taking the *ACT*.

- **Replace, in your mind, long hard story character names, like Jedidiah, Beauregard, Shaneequa…with Bill or Jane.**
  You can get lost in the names and it can draw your attention away from the question.

- **Read carefully!**
  Make sure you understand the main idea of the story. Ask yourself these two questions:
  1) What is the story about -- the subject?
  2) How does the subject of the story relate to the questions?

- **Review the basic concepts** — arithmetic operations and their order in solving problems, algebraic formulas, etc.

- **Prepare yourself by studying a few days of basic math formulas** a week before the test. (Example: $A = bh_2$)

- **Know a bit about word problems** and how to apply basic formulas to them.

- **Know how to solve 2-D and 3-D shape problems** involving circumference, perimeter, and area.

- **Be prepared for lots of questions using algebra.** (Example: 2x = 4 or xy = 0).

- **Be aware that a few questions may include seldom-used units of measurement,** such as "stones." The key is to use "proportion." Do not worry about the unit. (Example: If 100 bags of sand weigh 300 stones, how much would 170 bags weigh? Simply cross multiply to find "x.")

- **Bring a graphing calculator.**
  It will help in converting decimals to fractions and vice versa, with square root, etc., and will save a lot of time.

To Guess or Not to Guess?

As mentioned above, the question of taking a guess on a response to the *SAT Reasoning Test* is a common one. While some would say that guessing is a waste of time since **there is a .25 penalty for each wrong answer**, many would agree that you should **guess if you can eliminate at least one wrong answer before choosing a response**. In fact, guessing wisely can afford you at least partial credit for the response. Also, remember that **there is no penalty for guessing on grid-in* questions**.

* Math questions in which you have to fill in your own answer.

Some Final Thoughts

In addition to Nora's comments and our discussion on guessing, other general test-taking advice includes the following:
- **Get a good night's sleep before the test.**
- **Eat a light breakfast.**
- **Dress comfortably.**
- **Bring several sharpened #2 pencils and a good eraser.**
- **Arrive at the test site early or on time.**
  (You will not be allowed to take the test if you are late!)
- **Bring a snack and something to drink for break times.**

By utilizing these tips and strategies along with those offered in Chapters 3 and 4, you will increase your chances for success in taking the *SAT Reasoning Test*. So jump right in, review the comments provided in this guide, play the CD game, and have fun preparing for the *SAT*.

Chapter Three: Verbal Skills Review

Vocabulary

In Chapter Two, we offered you some tips for taking the *SAT Reasoning Test*, including ways to keep from getting tricked by the questions. In this chapter, we want to give you insight into figuring out the verbal sections of the exam. The bottom line is this: **If you're going to be successful on this part of the test, you have to know more than how to attack the questions**. You must know the meaning of the words in the reading passages and in the sentences you will be asked to complete!

We could give you a huge list of vocabulary words to memorize, but let's be honest, you won't memorize them. Even if you do memorize them, you'll still only know the words on the list. The very best way to learn vocabulary is to **READ EXTENSIVELY**. However, this is a crash course, so reading extensively between now and the test date is basically out of the question. Instead, let's focus on what you can do to score well on the verbal sections of the test.

The next best (and quickest) way to learn vocabulary is to review root words, prefixes, and suffixes. Although not every word that appears on the *SAT* has a recognizable root, knowing root words will still help you figure out some of the words that you don't know. You won't know every word on the test anyway. The test writers design it that way! Peruse the prefixes, suffixes, and root words in the following charts. Thinking of a word you already know that uses each prefix, suffix, or root may help you understand what the word on the test means.

A Root is Worth a Thousand Words

ROOT	MEANING
acerb	bitter
ag, act	drive, urge, act
agon	contest, struggle
alt	high
amic	friend
anim, anima	1. life 2. mind, soul, spirit
arch	rule, govern
aug, auct	increase
autrui	other people
ban	to command
bel, bell	1. fair, fine 2. war
bene	well
brev	short
cad, cas	fall
cand	glow, burn
cap, cip, cep	to take
ced, cess	go, yield
cens	give opinion, appraise
chron	time

ROOT	MEANING
ciarl	prattle, babble
cit, citat	arouse, summon, call out
clam, claim	call out
clement	lenient, mild
concili	bring together
copi	abundance
cor, cord	heart
corp	body
corrig	to correct
cred	believe, make trust
crit	a judge
cur	care, attention
curr, curs	run
cycl	circle, wheel
deleter	destroyer
derm	skin
didact	to teach
dol	grieve, worry
don	gift, give
dyn	power
enigm	riddle
equ	1. equal 2. horse
erro, erron	wanderer
exter, extra	beyond, outside
fac, fact, fec	make, form, act, do
fall, fals	err, beguile, deceive
fam	1. hunger 2. report
fastidi	loathing
ferv	boil
firm	steadfast, firm, strong
flagr	burn
flex, flect	bend
fund, fus	pour, melt
garr	chatter
gen, gener	origin, race, species
geo	earth
ger	bear, carry, rule
graph, gram	to write
grav	heavy
greg	flock, herd
gyro	turn
helio	sun
hemera	day
hibit	have, hold

ROOT	MEANING
host, hosp	host, guest
humil	humble
hydr	water
inan	void, empty
it, itiner	to go, journey
judic	judge
jur	1. swear 2. law, right
labor	to work
langu	be weak
leg, legis	1. appoint, send 2. law
leth	oblivion
lev	1. light 2. lift, raise, rise
line	line
listen	desire
liter	letter
log	speech, word, reason
loqu, locut	speak, talk
luc	1. shine 2. light
lud, lus	sport, play, laugh, mock
luna	moon
magn	great
mal	bad, ill
malle	hammer
man	hand
mar, mer	sea
mater, matr	maternal
metr, meter	measure
metus	fear
minn, minut	diminish, lessen
miser	miserable
mitt, miss	to send, let go
mor, mos	will
mord, mors	bite
morph	form, shape
mut	change
nat	1. born 2. swim
nav, naus	ship
noc	hurt, harm
nounce	bring tidings, tell
nov	new
omin	omen
oper	to work
ox	poison
pac	peace

ROOT	MEANING
pais	peace
par	1. equal 2. get ready, set
pars, part, partit	divide, share, separate, part
part	father
pat, pass	suffer, feel, endure
path	feel, suffer
pauc	little
ped	1. boy, child 2. foot
pell, puls	1. drive, urge 2. skin, fur
pet, petit	to seek
phan	to show
phem	speech
phone	voice, sound
pi	1. appease 2. devout
plac	please
plaud, plaus	clap hands
ple, plet	fill
plic	fold, bend, embrace
potent	powerful
povre	poor
prehend, prehens	take, seize, grasp
prob, prov	test
prodigi	token, omen
prol	offspring, increase
pud	feel shame, blush
put	1. think 2. cleanse, lop off
quiesc	rest, become quiet
quir, quer	to ask, seek
rat	think, calculate, settle
rect	ruled, right, straight
rept	creep
riv	stream
rog, rogat	ask, demand
rupt	to break
sanct	holy
scind	to cut
scrib, script	write
scrut	search into carefully
sent, sens	perceive, feel, think
sequi	to follow
serv	serve, keep
solemn	religious
solv, solut	loosen
son	sound

ROOT	MEANING
spec, spect	look, see, appear
spond, spons	promise, answer
stat	stand, standing
stru, struct	to build
suav	sweet
sume, sump	take, use, waste
surrect, surreg	rise
syc	fig
tac	be silent
tedi	irksomeness, irritating
ten, tend, tent	hold, stretch, strain
termin	boundary, end
the	1. a god 2. place, put
trepid	trembling, agitated
tric	hindrances, wiles, snares
trit	rub
trud, trus	thrust
turb	disturb, drive
un	one
ven, vent	to come
ver	1. spring 2. true, truth
verb	word
vert, vers	turn
vi	way, road
vir	1. man 2. poison
viv	life, to live
voc	1. voice 2. call
vol	1. wish, will 2. fly

Important Prefixes and Suffixes

PREFIX	SUFFIX	MEANING
a		without, not; to, toward, into, at; from; out; off; on
ab, abs		from, away
ad, ac, af, ag, al, am, an, ap, ar, as, at		to, toward, before, near
ana		up, back, again
ante		before
anti, contra, counter		against
apo		from, off
arch, archi		chief
auto, aut		self, same, automatic
be		to cause
bi		two, both, double
bio		life
cata		down, thoroughly
con, com, col, co, cor		together, with
de		down, from
deca, dec, deka, dek		ten
di		double
dia		through, between, across
dis		apart, away, un
epi		upon, to, besides
eu		good
ex, e, ec, ef, exo		out, out of
for		intensely, utterly
hyper		over
in, ir, el, em, en, il, im		in, into
inter		between
mal		bad
meta		among, with, after, over
mis		wrongly, ill
mono		single, sole
multi		many
ob, oc, of, op		to, toward, before
octa		eight
over		above; superior; excessively
pan, omni		all
par, per		through
para		beside
peri		around, about
poly		many

port, pros		toward
post		after, behind
preter		beyond
pro, pur, pre		before, forward
proto		first
quadri, quadr, quadra, quadru		four, square
re, red, ana		back, again
se		aside, apart
se, sed, de, des, dis		away, apart
semi		half
sub, suc, suf, sum, sup, sur, sus		under, after
super, supra		above, over, beyond
syl, sym, syn		together
tra, trans		beyond, across
tri		three
un		reverse
un, non, ir, in, il, im		not
uni		one
	able, ible	able, capable (makes words into adjectives)
	al	referring (makes words into adjectives)
	ary, ory	place where (turns words into nouns)
	cle, cule	small
	ed	makes a regular verb past tense
	er	makes the comparative degree
	er, or	one who performs a specific action
	est	makes the superlative degree
	fy, ate	to make (turns words into verbs)
	ing	makes present participle form of verbs
	ist	one who, that which
	ive	inclined to (makes words into adjectives)
	ly	like, resembling
	or, ant, ar, ist, an, ian, ent	one who (turns words into nouns)
	ous	full of (makes words into adjectives)
	phobia	excessive fear
	s, es	makes a word plural
	sion, tion, ancy, ment, ency, ty, ance, ence, ity	the state of, the act of (makes words into nouns)
	y, ey	like, full of (makes words into adjectives)

If you really want to memorize a long list of words that may or may not appear on the test, there are plenty of lists available. One of the best ones is *The Hipp List* by IVY1600, Inc. (*www.ivy1600.com*). Or you can get help in learning the words in context by reading *Tooth and Nail: A Novel*

Approach, by Charles Harrington Elster and Joseph Elliott — a fictional work that incorporates, in its plot, the most common vocabulary words appearing in *SAT* tests. But learning vocabulary through etymology and an understanding of prefixes and suffixes is essential to success on the *SAT Reasoning Test*.

Try these practice questions:

1. The ___ of the football players was unfounded as their team lost in the first round.

   A. conflagration
   B. fervor
   C. insolence
   D. autonomy
   E. humility

The **correct answer is C**. The players had **insolence (excessive pride)**, but it was unfounded because they didn't win a single game. Even though you can't use the root chart to figure out the meaning of insolence, you CAN use it to figure out the meanings of the other words and thereby eliminate them as choices. Choice A (conflagration: a large, destructive fire) makes no sense at all. Choice E (humility: disposition to be humble) is the opposite of what we need. Feelings of humility would be **founded**, not **unfounded**. Don't let choices B (fervor: intensity of feeling) and D (autonomy: independence, freedom) trick you. The players could have intense feelings and independence, regardless of their success.

2. Sarah Beth, ___ and ___, was always sure to be invited to parties.

   A. gregarious . . . amiable
   B. aloof . . . reserved
   C. outgoing . . . reticent
   D. supercilious . . . altruistic
   E. antediluvian . . . burgeoning

The **correct answer is A**. The word *and* tells us we're looking for synonyms. A person who is gregarious (sociable, enjoying company) and amiable (friendly, sociable) would be welcome at any party. Aloof and reserved (choice B) are synonyms as well, but no one would want an indifferent and standoffish person at a party. Choices C and D present opposites, and choice E provides words that don't even describe a person.

More Practice Questions

1. I would rather have a boss who is ___ than one who ___ all the time.

    A. generous . . . bequeaths
    B. irascible . . . argues
    C. consistent . . . vacillates
    D. garrulous . . . talks
    E. nostalgic . . . reminisces

2. Even though our principal can't ___ senior pranks, he usually ___ them.

    A. sanction . . . condones
    B. elucidate . . . clarifies
    C. vindicate . . . criticizes
    D. thwart . . . foils
    E. revere . . . acclaims

3. Although we never have any extra money, we are by no means ___.

    A. affluent
    B. indigent
    C. rejuvenated
    D. altruistic
    E. optimistic

4. I trained ___ for the race, but my energy still ___ in the last mile.

    A. arduously . . . intensified
    B. resolutely . . . aggrandized
    C. lackadaisically . . . atrophied
    D. casually . . . waned
    E. diligently . . . flagged

5. I have nothing but admiration for the ___ and insightful professor.

    A. abstract
    B. lax
    C. obtuse
    D. naive
    E. sagacious

6. Many people criticize Jackson's poetry; I must agree that it is rather ___.

   A. eloquent
   B. demiurgic
   C. pedestrian
   D. picturesque
   E. aesthetic

7. Even when I disagree with my parents' rules, I find it's wise to ___.

   A. chastise
   B. digress
   C. augment
   D. acquiesce
   E. amass

8. Megan's campaign speech was so ___ that it sounded more like a ___ than a political platform.

   A. inquisitive . . . tirade
   B. vitriolic . . . diatribe
   C. verbose . . . satire
   D. candid . . . manifesto
   E. reticent . . . sermon

9. Austin's ideas were usually fabulous even if they were a little ___.

   A. quixotic
   B. mundane
   C. legitimate
   D. heinous
   E. prodigious

10. A more ___ ruler would have made an effort to ___ the suffering of his people.

    A. formidable . . . relieve
    B. benevolent . . . alleviate
    C. kind-hearted . . . burgeon
    D. apathetic . . . assuage
    E. magnanimous . . . augment

Answers to Vocabulary Practice Questions:

1. **C.** The words *rather* and *than* suggest that we're looking for opposites. All of the answer choices in this set are synonyms except for *consistent* and *vacillates* (or changes from one opinion to another).

2. **A.** He can't approve senior pranks, but he does overlook them. *Even though* suggests that we're looking for words that are opposites or nearly opposites. Choices B, D, and E do not contain opposites. Choice C doesn't work because a prank can't be vindicated, or proven innocent.

3. **B.** The word *although* suggests that we're looking for a word that means the opposite of never having any extra money (having lots!). Watch out for the two negative words, though (*never* and *no*). Although we don't have extra, we are *not* poor, or indigent.

4. **E.** The word *but* signals a contrast. I trained hard (diligently), but my energy ran out (flagged) anyway. Remember that the test writers like to use familiar words (like *flag*) in unfamiliar ways.

5. **E.** The word *and* indicates that we're looking for a synonym or near synonym of *insightful*. Watch out for the words *nothing but*, though. This grammatically acceptable double negative means that I *do* have admiration, so we're looking for an admirable trait. Only *sagacious*, or wise, fits the bill.

6. **C.** Because *I agree*, we're looking for a word that criticizes the poetry. *Pedestrian*, another familiar word used in an unfamiliar way, means dull or ordinary.

7. **D.** This sentence calls for an opposite or near opposite of *disagree*. Even when I don't agree, I still give in, or *acquiesce*.

8. **B.** The words *so* and *that* indicate a cause and effect. Since the speech was *vitriolic* (burning and caustic), the speech came across as a *diatribe* (a bitter, critical speech). The only other word pair that shows a logical cause-and-effect relationship is choice D, but *manifesto* doesn't contrast with *political statement*.

9. **A.** Again, *even if* shows contrast, but the word *little* suggests that we're not looking for an antonym of *fabulous*. Austin's ideas may be fabulous, but they're extremely idealistic, or *quixotic*.

10. **B.** This sentence calls for a cause-and-effect relationship. A benevolent (or generous and charitable) ruler would alleviate (or lessen) suffering. The other answer choices don't show a logical cause-and-effect relationship.

Critical Reading

Many students who have taken the *SAT* will tell you that the critical reading section is the most difficult part of the exam. Why? It is because the lengthy passages require you to stay focused! In order to stay awake and to concentrate during the critical reading section of the *SAT*, you must remember **one important rule: Stay engaged with the text. In other words, interact with the passages in front of you.**

Here's how:

First, **write on the passage**. Underline information that you think may be important. **Underline transitional or signal words** such as *however, therefore, since, nevertheless,* and *above all*. Circle words that are unfamiliar to you. *Put stars next to examples* the author provides. **Make brief notes in the margins** about the author's purpose, point, or attitude. Writing on the passage serves three important purposes. It helps you to make more sense of what you're reading; it helps you to remember what you've read; and (here's the clincher) it helps you to stay tuned in while you're reading!

The **second way to stay engaged** with the text is **to keep a conversation going in your head while you're reading**. Go ahead. No one else will know. Talk back to the author of the passage. Ask him questions like "What point are you trying to make?" or "Why did you describe the situation that way?" Make accusations like "Wow, you obviously don't like this character very much" or "Well, I can tell you think global warming is nothing but a scam." Get inside his head by saying "You're trying to be sarcastic, aren't you?" or "Oh, I see where you're going with this example." These conversations may feel awkward at first, but good readers have them all the time. They help you to think like the author (which means you'll have an easier time answering the questions), and they help you to (once again) stay tuned in to the reading!

Although interacting with the passages is important, **keep in mind that you have a time limit**: so don't get too carried away. Go **through the passage one time, marking it and talking to it as you go**. Don't dwell on any one aspect of the passage. Then **go to the questions. Read through each one, and answer the ones you know first. Then go back to the ones about which you are unsure. When you're going back to the passage to figure these out, keep this in mind: Generally, the questions follow the order of the passage.** In other words, you should be able to find the answer to the first question near the beginning of the passage. The last questions, however, will pertain to the passage as a whole.

On both the long and short passages, you will see the same types of questions. You'll have to answer questions about the author's point and how the author uses his words to make that point. Specifically, you need practice in figuring out a passage's main idea, the author's attitude or tone toward the subject matter, and what the passage implies (says indirectly or between the lines). You'll also need to be able to compare and contrast aspects of the double-passage questions. Sometimes you will be asked to figure out the meaning of a word in context. In this case, the question will give you the line location of the word. Perhaps you will have already identified the word as one that is unfamiliar to you. Either way, you'll need to read the sentence (and possibly the ones immediately before and after it) and look for context clues—words in the sentence that give away the meaning of the target word.

Finally, some questions will refer to literary terms. A quick review of the following terms may be helpful:

Alliteration: repetition of sounds at the beginning of words (cowering in the corner of their cages)

Allusion: a reference to something commonly known (If it continues to rain, we will have to build an ark.)

Assonance: repetition of vowel sounds within words (rode through the snow)

Cliché: a trite, overused expression (as pretty as a picture)

Foreshadowing: hinting at what is to come

Hyperbole: an exaggeration (I ate so much dessert that I probably gained a hundred pounds!)

Imagery: description that appeals to the senses (dry leaves crunching underfoot like broken glass)

Irony: incongruity between what is expected and what occurs or between what is said and what is meant (a butcher who is a vegetarian)

Metaphor: a direct comparison in which one thing represents another (the world is a stage)

Motif: a recurring subject, theme, or idea

Onomatopoeia: the use of words that imitate sounds (swish, pop, buzz)

Oxymoron: a pairing of contradictory terms (deafening silence)

Paradox: a statement that seems self-contradictory (less is more)

Personification: giving human characteristics to inanimate objects (daffodils danced in the breeze)

Pun: humorous use of words that sound alike but have different meanings (Will the mayor be re-elected? He "mayor" may not!)

Rhetorical Question: question meant to make a point, not to be answered (What's the point of having the rule if it isn't enforced?)

Sarcasm: harsh or bitter irony (telling someone who is always late, "Oh, I see you're on time as usual.")

Simile: a comparison that uses like or as (as sweet as honey)

Symbol: something used to represent something else

Theme: the main or unifying idea (loneliness, forgiveness, love)

Tone: author's attitude toward his subject (approval, pride, resentment)

Try reading the passage below and answering the questions that follow it. Although it is shorter than an actual *SAT* passage, the following excerpt will provide good practice:

The United States and Canadian governments are mounting a defense against a Russian invasion. No, the clock has not been turned back. These invaders are Asian gypsy moths, foliage-chomping insects that can cause billions of dollars in damage. Experts believe they entered North America from Russia last year in egg masses attached to grain vessels. The larger Asian gypsy moth is a more voracious feeder than the common North American strain and can feed on Pacific Northwest tree species. Unlike the flightless North American female, an Asian female can fly 20 miles between mating and egg-laying. The United States Health Inspection Service is barring from West Coast ports ships found carrying egg masses. The Tacoma and Portland areas, as well as Vancouver, British Columbia, have been sprayed with a biopesticide.

(National Geographic, July 1992)

1. The author of this passage refers to the increase in Asian gypsy moths as a "Russian invasion" in order to

    A. make a political statement.
    B. stress the severity of the problem.
    C. warn readers about underhanded activities of the Russian government.
    D. make light of a serious situation.
    E. demonstrate his distaste for all moths.

The **correct answer** to this question is **B**. By comparing the moth problem to a well-known historical situation, the author emphasizes the severity of the increase in the Asian gypsy moth population. Let's take a look at the other choices. Choice A might trick some test-takers because the comparison is political in nature. However, the rest of the passage doesn't deal with political matters at all. Choice C is incorrect for the same reason. Given the information the author provides in the passage, we can be certain that he isn't making light of the situation (D), and he never even mentions other types of moths (E).

2. Based on its use in the passage, the word *voracious* (line 5) most likely means

    A. speedy.
    B. able to go days without eating.
    C. picky.
    D. consuming large amounts of food.
    E. meat-eating.

The **correct answer** to this question is **D**. The Asian gypsy moth is a threat because it eats so much. The word *larger* is a good context clue because it suggests that these moths eat more than do common North American moths.

3. Which group of words from the passage best reflects the writer's tone?

    A. mounting, barring, sprayed
    B. egg masses, mating, egg-laying
    C. invaders, foliage-chomping, voracious
    D. Canadian, Russian, Asian, North American
    E. larger, common, feeder

The **correct answer** is **C**. We're looking for subjective words here--words that the author chooses to express his attitude. Because the writer uses words like *invaders, foliage-chomping*, and *voracious*, we can tell that he is clearly concerned about this problem. Choices B, D, and E offer purely objective words. The words *mounting* and *barring* in choice A seem tempting, but *sprayed* doesn't fit the bill.

More Practice Questions

I. This passage is excerpted from a 1986 article about the use of social studies textbooks in elementary schools.

The inherent difficulty of social studies content stems mainly from the heavy technical concept load of social studies textbook passages. Technical concepts are one- or two-word "ideas" which have specialized meaning in social studies (for example: government, delta, immigrants, interdependence, economy, constitution, federal, cotton belt, division of labor, and political party). These words may have little or no meaning for students unless specific vocabulary or concept development lessons precede their first encounter with such terms. Yet basal social studies textbooks are notorious for heavy technical concept load and "thin" discussion of topics, making even the most careful independent reading low in potential benefit.

Hard-to-pronounce names of cities, faraway countries, and foreign language names contribute to the complexity of textbook content. Many adult readers are stopped by these words, yet social studies is neither complete nor accurate without them.

Add to the above problems frequent references to long periods of time or huge distances, and it becomes even more apparent why children have trouble learning from their social studies textbooks. What must a child of 9 or 10 think when the book says, "Our country was founded over 200 years ago"--or perhaps worse, "long, long ago"? What do expressions such as "far to the north," or "over a thousand miles to the east," mean to students who are not sure which direction is which and who have never traveled further than across the state or out of town?

1. The word *inherent* (line 1) means

    A. naturally occurring.
    B. worst.
    C. least important.
    D. intentional.
    E. minor.

2. According to the author of this passage, which of the following does not contribute to the ineffectiveness of social studies textbooks?

    A. difficult terminology
    B. references to long periods of time
    C. uninteresting topics
    D. words that are difficult to pronounce
    E. skimpy explanations of topics

3. The author's main argument is that

    A. social studies texts have no place in the classroom.
    B. social studies texts should be rewritten so that they are easier to understand.
    C. children today are not as intelligent as children in the past.
    D. the difficulties of social studies texts are necessary hurdles that must be overcome.
    E. the authors of social studies texts know nothing about children.

4. In the last paragraph of the passage, the author drives his point home with

    A. rhetorical questions.
    B. imagery.
    C. hyperboles.
    D. symbolism.
    E. an oxymoron.

II. This passage is excerpted from a 2003 article about the impact of electronic communication on writing.

Word processing and e-publishing have brought about interesting developments in the way writers write. In general, the malleable nature of electronic text has made the physical process of composing more "elastic" in that writers are quicker to commit thought to writing and to reorganize content because it is simple to make changes on the electronic screen. Even young children find it easy to insert and manipulate images and video or audio clips in their texts. In addition, writers who publish on the Web perceive it as a new rhetorical space that provides options for using non-linear, alternative structures, making it necessary for them to anticipate how audiences might physically navigate through their hypertext compositions. This consciousness creates complex perspectives and a heightened awareness of traditional rhetorical elements in a way that text alone never could.

5. The word "malleable" (line 2) means

   A. inflexible.
   B. simplistic.
   C. pliable.
   D. insincere.
   E. complex.

6. The author of this passage suggests that word processing and e-publishing have made the writing and reading of text

   A. more complex than ever before.
   B. quicker than ever before.
   C. more simple than ever before.
   D. more decorative than ever before.
   E. more organized than ever before.

III. This passage is excerpted from a 2002 article about ecosystems.

When someone asks us where we are from or what we do, most of us mention the town or city where we live, our occupation, where we attended school, or our family heritage. We respond in terms of human communities, cultures, and geopolitical boundaries. We seldom, if ever, describe ourselves in terms of our ecological status in the natural world. We humans have so completely ordered, designed, and defined our physical environs and social milieu that our ecological connections have slipped from consciousness. Perhaps this is why we seem so unaware of our impact on nature and our rapid destruction of natural systems. We simply do not perceive ourselves as being part of the natural order of beings.

All of us live within ecological systems, or "ecosystems," and through our commerce, food distribution, and use of natural resources we each indirectly participate in the custodianship of many ecosystems worldwide. Ironically, we are simultaneously the most potent forces within most ecosystems, and yet nearly oblivious to the ecological effects of our daily lifestyles. There has never been a time when a deep understanding of ecosystems and our roles within them has been more critical. Indeed, the world's freshwater ecosystems are so degraded that their ability to support plant and animal life, including humans, is viewed by many as being in peril. Learning about ecosystems is more than an expected focus in biology classes; it has become a study in survival.

Ecosystems are functional units of interacting abiotic, biotic, and cultural (anthropogenic) components. All natural ecosystems are open systems where energy and matter are transferred in and out through the complex interactions of energy, water, carbon, oxygen, nitrogen, phosphorus, sulfur, and other cycles. Unfortunately, many scientists contend, we humans have disrupted the balance of transfers across ecosystem boundaries. In addition to learning our place within ecosystems, we must learn to become better stewards and managers of ecosystems.

7. The author's tone in this passage can best be described as

    A. apologetic.
    B. scolding.
    C. warning.
    D. encouraging.
    E. unconcerned.

8. The first two sentences of this passage are primarily intended to

    A. capture the reader's attention with an anecdote.
    B. demonstrate our unawareness of our place in the natural world.
    C. cause the reader to think about his or her own role in society.
    D. emphasize the importance of a person's background.
    E. show ways in which we are all different.

9. The author's attitude in this passage is represented by all of the following phrases except

    A. "must learn to become better stewards and managers of ecosystems."
    B. "oblivious to the ecological effects of our daily lifestyles."
    C. "rapid destruction of natural systems."
    D. "indirectly participate in the custodianship of many ecosystems worldwide."
    E. "disrupted the balance of transfers across ecosystem boundaries."

IV. This passage is excerpted from a 1922 novel about a Midwestern American's journey to the front of World War I.

Claude backed the little Ford car out of its shed, ran it up to the horse-tank, and began to throw water on the mud-crusted wheels and windshield. While he was at work the two hired men, Dan and Jerry, came shambling down the hill to feed the stock. Jerry was grumbling and swearing about something, but Claude wrung out his wet rags and, beyond a nod, paid no attention to them. Somehow his father always managed to have the roughest and dirtiest hired men in the country working for him. Claude had a grievance against Jerry just now, because of his treatment of one of the horses.

Molly was a faithful old mare, the mother of many colts; Claude and his younger brother had learned to ride on her. This man Jerry, taking her out to work one morning, let her step on a board with a nail sticking up in it. He pulled the nail out of her foot, said nothing to anybody, and drove her to the cultivator all day. Now she had been standing in her stall for weeks, patiently suffering, her body wretchedly thin, and her leg swollen until it looked like an elephant's. She would have to stand there, the veterinary said, until her hoof came off and she grew a new one, and she would always be stiff. Jerry had not been discharged, and he exhibited the poor animal as if she were a credit to him.

Mahailey came out on the hilltop and rang the breakfast bell. After the hired men went up to the house, Claude slipped into the barn to see that Molly had got her share of oats. She was eating quietly, her head hanging, and her scaly, dead-looking foot lifted just a little from the ground. When he stroked her neck and talked to her she stopped grinding and gazed at him mournfully. She knew him, and wrinkled her nose and drew her upper lip back from her worn teeth, to show that she liked being petted. She let him touch her foot and examine her leg.

When Claude reached the kitchen, his mother was sitting at one end of the breakfast table, pouring weak coffee, his brother and Dan and Jerry were in their chairs, and Mahailey was baking griddle cakes at the stove. A moment later Mr. Wheeler came down the enclosed stairway and walked the length of the table to his own place. He was a very large man, taller and broader than any of his neighbors. He seldom wore a coat in summer, and his rumpled shirt bulged out carelessly over the belt of his trousers. His florid face was clean shaven, likely to be a trifle tobacco-stained about the mouth, and it was conspicuous both for good-nature and coarse humour, and for an imperturbable physical composure. Nobody in the county had ever seen Nat Wheeler flustered about anything, and nobody had ever heard him speak with complete seriousness. He kept up his easy-going, jocular affability even with his own family.

As soon as he was seated, Mr. Wheeler reached for the two-pint sugar bowl and began to pour sugar into his coffee. Ralph asked him if he were going to the circus. Mr. Wheeler winked. "I shouldn't wonder if I happened in town sometime before the elephants get away." He spoke very deliberately, with a State-of-Maine drawl, and his voice was smooth and agreeable. "You boys better start in early, though. You can take the wagon and the mules, and load in the cowhides. The butcher has agreed to take them."

Claude put down his knife. "Can't we have the car? I've washed it on purpose."

"And what about Dan and Jerry? They want to see the circus just as much as you do, and I want the hides should go in; they're bringing a good price now. I don't mind about your washing the car; mud preserves the paint, they say, but it'll be all right this time, Claude."

10. Claude's attitude toward Jerry is one of

    A. respect.
    B. resentment.
    C. jealousy.
    D. camaraderie.
    E. indifference.

11. The expression "imperturbable physical composure" (paragraph 4, line 9) suggests that Nat Wheeler

    A. has a hard time keeping his face clean.
    B. is terribly overweight.
    C. cannot be irritated.
    D. is always in a great mood.
    E. always appears calm by his facial expressions.

12. Which statement by Mr. Wheeler represents an example of verbal irony?

    A. "You can take the wagon and the mules, and load in the cowhides."
    B. "I shouldn't wonder if I happened in town sometime before the elephants get away."
    C. "They want to see the circus just as much as you do, and I want the hides should go in; they're bringing a good price now."
    D. "I don't mind about your washing the car; mud preserves the paint, they say, but it'll be all right this time, Claude."
    E. "And what about Dan and Jerry?"

Answers to Critical Reading Practice Questions

1. **A.** Because of the highly technical language of social studies, the difficult terminology discussed in this paragraph is a naturally occurring problem.

2. **C.** The passage specifically mentions all of the other problems, but at no time does the author suggest that social studies is not interesting.

3. **D.** The author states that the difficulties of the texts are inherent (or natural) and that social studies texts would be "neither complete nor accurate without" difficult words. Rather than passing judgment on the texts or on their authors, the author identifies necessary hurdles that must be overcome.

4. **A.** The author uses two rhetorical questions, or questions meant to make a point rather than to be answered.

5. **C.** The word "elastic" provides a good context clue, as does the statement that "it is simple to make changes on the electronic screen." The word "malleable" suggests that the words on the screen are pliable, or can be easily altered.

6. **A.** This question is a little tricky because the author utilizes many of the words that are in the wrong answer choices (such as *quicker, simple,* and *reorganize*). None of these terms, however, represents his point. The use of alternative structures, images, and other nontraditional rhetorical elements makes electronic communication more complex than traditional texts.

7. **C.** The author is certainly not apologetic, encouraging, or unconcerned. Although some of his words seem scolding, his overall purpose is more to warn than to scold. Therefore, *warning* is a better choice than *scolding*.

8. **B.** Although the opening sentences of the passage may do any of the things listed in the answer choices, their intended purpose is to show that we are oblivious to our place in nature. The focus of the rest of the first paragraph reinforces this purpose.

9. **D.** All of the other answer choices contain negative words and phrases that warn of threats to ecosystems.

10. **B.** Claude resents Jerry because Jerry injured a horse that is special to Claude. Evidence of Claude's resentment can be seen in his description of Jerry's carelessness and of the horse's resulting injuries.

11. **E.** The sentence following the expression sums up its meaning: no one had ever seen Mr. Wheeler flustered. Although C is also a tempting choice, the author doesn't say that Mr. Wheeler can't be irritated, just that he never looks irritated.

12. **D.** Verbal irony involves saying the opposite of what you really mean. Mr. Wheeler teases Claude by suggesting that he would rather have a dirty car.

We suggest that you re-read the sample questions and the rationale behind arriving at the correct response several times to be sure that you understand the concepts fully. As you play the CD game and take the practice tests, try to remember the things you have learned about tackling these two types of reading questions on the *SAT*.

Writing

The writing portion of the *SAT Reasoning Test* involves both responding to multiple-choice questions and writing a brief essay. Interestingly, it consists, mostly, of multiple choice questions! And they're tough ones at that! Therefore, only the most grammar-savvy students should face this section of the test without some grammar review.

Here is the lowdown on the most popular types of issues you'll encounter on this part of the test:

Subject/verb agreement

This is by far the test writers' favorite type of question. It is important that your subjects agree with your verbs. In other words, you must write *he jumps* instead of *he jump* because a singular subject (*he*) takes a singular verb (*jumps*). Subject/verb agreement gets tricky when a prepositional phrase comes between the subject and the verb. However, you should ignore the prepositional phrase and make the verb agree with the subject. (One of the girls likes the movie.) Note that the following pronouns are singular: *each, either, neither, someone, somebody, everyone, everybody, anyone, anybody, no one, nobody*. (Neither of the movies was very good.) When two or more subjects are joined by *and*, you must use a plural verb. (Hiking and camping are fun.) When two or more subjects are joined by *or* or *nor*, the verb agrees with the subject nearest the verb. (Neither the *players nor the coach is* late for practice.) Finally, amounts are usually singular, as are titles. (*Two hours* is a long time to wait. *Great Expectations* is a great book.)

Identify the error in the sentence below:

<u>Help</u> <u>for improving</u> test-taking skills <u>and reading skills</u> <u>are</u> also available. <u>no error</u>
  a   b   c   d   e

The **correct answer is D**. The subject (*Help*) is singular and therefore requires a singular verb (*is*, not *are*). The prepositional phrase (*for improving test-taking skills and reading skills*) is meant to trick you because it's plural. It's also long so that by the time you reach the verb, you've lost track of the subject, so be careful!

Pronoun/antecedent agreement

This concept is very similar to subject/verb agreement and is another favorite of the test writers. A noun that a pronoun refers to is called its antecedent. For example, in the sentence, *The boy rode his bike*, **boy** is the **antecedent of the pronoun *his***. Just as a subject has to agree with its verb, a pronoun has to agree with its antecedent. If the antecedent is singular, the pronoun must be singular; if the antecedent is plural, the pronoun must be plural. Pronoun/antecedent agreement also gets tricky when the antecedent is followed by a prepositional phrase. However, you should ignore the prepositional phrase and make the pronoun agree with the antecedent. (One of the girls forgot her pencil.) Note that the following pronouns are singular: *each, either, neither, someone, somebody, everyone, everybody, anyone, anybody, no one, nobody*. (Neither of the players remembered to tie his shoes.) When two or more antecedents are joined by *and*, you must use a plural pronoun. (Katianne and Ralston took off their shoes.) When two or more antecedents are joined by *or* or *nor*, the pronoun agrees with the antecedent closest to it. (Neither the players nor the coach brought his stopwatch.)

Identify the error in the sentence below:

If a <u>student</u> wishes <u>to be involved</u> in the class, <u>they</u> must get <u>parental consent</u> first. <u>no error</u>
        a   b   c   d   e

The **correct answer is C**. The antecedent of the pronoun is *student*, which is singular. Therefore, the pronoun must be singular as well (*he* or *she* rather than *they*).

Parallel structure

When you join two or more ideas—in the form of words, phrases, or even clauses—in a sentence (usually with the help of a conjunction), the ideas you join must be parallel. In other words, the grammatical structure of each one must be the same. For example, *Michelle is kind, helpful, and likes puppies* is not parallel because we're joining two adjectives (*kind* and *helpful*) and one verb (*likes*). To correct the sentence, you could write *Michelle is kind, is helpful, and likes puppies* (three verbs) or *Michelle is kind, helpful, and loving* (three adjectives).

Try this practice question:

Lucie is not only a loving <u>character, but she is a strong character as well</u>.
    A. character, but she is a strong character as well
    B. character but she is a strong character as well
    C. character, but she is also a strong character
    D. character but also a strong character
    E. character, in addition to that she is also very strong

The **correct answer is D**. In the original sentence, an adjective and noun follow the *not only* part of the correlating conjunction, but a subject and verb follow the *but* part of the correlating conjunction. Instead, we need an adjective and noun to follow *but*. Note that the correct answer is also the shortest, as is often the case in the "improving sentences" questions.

Passive voice

Although passive voice isn't grammatically incorrect, it's often stylistically unpleasant. Passive voice consists of a *to be* verb (*is, be, am, are, was, were, been, being*) and a past participle (such as *stolen, pushed,* or *enjoyed*). The subject of the passive voice verb is receiving the action rather than doing the action. For example, *The play was enjoyed by the audience*. Although *play* is the subject, the object of the preposition (*audience*) is actually doing the enjoying. The sentence would sound much better if it were active: *The audience enjoyed the play*. Not all past participles indicate passive voice, however.

For example, in the sentence *I have listened to that CD all day long, have listened* is not passive voice. Although there are some cases in which passive voice is acceptable, use active voice whenever possible. **Note that passive voice is not considered an error in the "identifying errors" questions, but you should watch for it in the "improving sentences" questions.**

Try this practice question:

The letter is written by Sir Andrew and Sir Toby as a trick to make a fool of Malvolio.

   A. The letter is written by Sir Andrew and Sir Toby
   B. Sir Andrew and Sir Toby write the letter
   C. The letter, which is written by Sir Andrew and Sir Toby,
   D. The letter having been written by Sir Andrew and Sir Toby
   E. Sir Andrew and Sir Toby are the authors of the letter used.

The **correct answer is B** because the subjects (*Sir Andrew and Sir Toby*) do the action (*write*). In other words, the sentence is in active voice rather than passive voice. While E is also active voice, it's wordy. Remember, on the *SAT* there may be more than one **correct** answer, but you're looking for the **best** one. Stay away from wordiness.

Use of modifiers

A modifier is a word that describes another word. Modifiers come in three degrees of comparison: positive (*tall, carefully*), comparative (*taller, more carefully*), and superlative (*tallest, most carefully*). Use the positive form when you're just describing something. (*Joe is tall.*) Use the comparative form when you're comparing two things. (*Joe is taller than John.*) Use the superlative form when you're comparing three or more things. (*Joe is the tallest person in his class.*) Avoid using an adjective to modify a verb. (*He ran quickly*, not *He ran quick*.) When you're comparing something with a group it belongs to, you must include the word *other* or the word *else*. (*This class is more fun than any other class. Mrs. Miller is nicer than anyone else I know.*) Finally, note that *less, amount*, and *much* refer to collective nouns (uncountable things like traffic and rain), while *fewer, number*, and *many* refer to nouns you can count (like cars and raindrops). A modifier is dangling when it refers to a word not directly stated in the sentence. A misplaced modifier is one that is in the wrong place in the sentence. Always put modifiers as close to the words they modify as possible. Otherwise, your sentences are unclear.

Try these practice questions:

1) When <u>you</u> captivate <u>the attention</u> of your audience, you <u>have</u> <u>less</u> conduct problems. <u>no error</u>
         a   b   c   d   e

The **correct answer is D**. Since you can count conduct problems, you must use *fewer* instead of *less*. Don't be tricked into choosing A. Although some high school teachers claim that you should never use first person pronouns (like *I*) or second person pronouns (like *you*) in your writing, that's not true at all. Although there are situations in which you should avoid first and second person pronouns, there are plenty of times when they're completely appropriate.

2) The sirens cause passing sailors to go completely insane by singing beautiful songs.

   A. The sirens cause passing sailors to go completely insane by singing beautiful songs.
   B. Singing beautiful songs, the sirens cause passing sailors to go completely insane.
   C. The sirens, which are always singing beautiful songs, cause sailors to go completely insane.
   D. Whenever they are singing beautiful songs, the sirens cause sailors to go completely insane.
   E. The sirens, who cause passing sailors to go completely insane, are always singing beautiful songs.

The **correct answer is B** because *singing beautiful songs* modifies the sirens. Choice A suggests that the sailors go insane by singing beautiful songs themselves! Choices C, D, and E are wordy and awkward.

Pronoun usage

We already talked about pronoun/antecedent agreement, but you must also know when to use which pronoun case (such as *I* versus *me*). You must use nominative pronouns (such as *I*, *he*, and *they*) for subjects and predicate nominatives. (*Jacob and I are studying for our math test.*) You must use objective pronouns (such as *me, her,* and *them*) for direct objects, indirect objects, and objects of prepositions. (*Will you eat lunch with Rudy and me?*) Most students have trouble deciding when to use *who* and when to use *whom*. Remember that *who* (nominative case) is for subjects and predicate nominatives. *Whom* (objective case) is for direct objects, indirect objects, and objects of prepositions. Also, remember that *hisself, theirselves,* and *themself* are not words.

Identify the error in the sentence below:

<u>Since</u> Mr. Key <u>wasn't sure</u> <u>who</u> was responsible, he gave both Lauren and <u>I</u> detention. <u>no error</u>
   a   b   c   d   e

The **correct answer is D**. You must use the objective pronoun *me* rather than the nominative pronoun *I* because *Lauren and me* is an indirect object. Don't be fooled by choice C. *Who* is correct because it acts as the subject of the clause *who was responsible*.

Verb tense

As a general rule, you should use past tense (*walked*) to write about something that happened in the past, present tense (*walks*) to write about something that is happening right now, and future tense (*will walk*) to write about something that hasn't yet happened. In a verb phrase, the tense is determined by the helping verb. For example, *has walked* is present perfect tense, but *had walked* is past perfect tense. Avoid switching verb tense within your writing. For example, if you're telling a story and using past tense, don't randomly switch to present tense.

Identify the error in the sentence below:

<u>When</u> Kyle comes over to my house, we <u>started</u> <u>playing</u> video games <u>immediately</u>. <u>no error</u>
  a   b   c   d   e

The **correct answer is B**. *Started* is a past tense verb, whereas *comes* is present tense. Note that *comes* and *started* aren't both underlined. If they were, it would be impossible to determine which one should be changed!

Verb usage

Sometimes you might use the right verb tense and correct subject/verb agreement, but you just use the wrong verb or verb form. Here are a few tips regarding verbs that people sometimes misuse: *Lie, sit*, and *rise* are all intransitive verbs and are therefore not followed by a direct object. (I like to *lie* under the tree.) *Lay, set*, and *raise* are transitive and therefore are followed by a direct object. (*Set* the books on the table.) *Shall* goes with *I* and *we* (I *shall* go to the movie.) *Will* goes with everyone else. (She *will* go to the movie.) Use *may* when you're referring to permission. (*May* I have that pencil?) Use *can* when you're referring to ability. (*Can* you run twelve miles?) Sometimes people use the wrong form of a verb. For example, a past tense verb (*spoke*) does not need a helping verb, but a past participle (*has spoken*) does.

Identify the error in the sentence below:

<u>On weekends</u> I like <u>to lay</u> around and <u>watch</u> movies. <u>no error</u>
      a   b   c   d   e

The **correct answer is B**. Here we have to use the intransitive verb *lie* rather than the transitive verb *lay* because we don't have a direct object. Although *around* may look like a direct object, it tells "where" rather than "what."

Run-on sentences

When you have two whole sentences stuck together with only a comma in between them, you have a type of run-on called a comma splice (such as *I'm starving, I hope we can eat soon*). A comma is not strong enough to hold two sentences together. You must add a coordinating conjunction (such as *I'm starving, so I hope we can eat soon*), change the comma to a semicolon (such as *I'm starving; I hope we can eat soon*), create two separate sentences (such as *I'm starving. I hope we can eat soon*), or reword the whole thing (such as *I hope we can eat soon because I'm starving*). When you have two whole sentences (or even more than two) stuck together with nothing at all in between them, you have a run-on sentence (such as *I'm starving I hope we can eat soon*). You can correct the run-on sentence the same way you correct the comma splice.

Try this practice question:

We have two hours to get <u>there, that's plenty of time.</u>

    A. there, that's plenty of time.
    B. there that's plenty of time.
    C. there, which is plenty of time.
    D. there, that should definitely be plenty of time.
    E. there, which certainly should be plenty of time.

The **correct answer is C**. Choices A and B are both run-on sentences. So is D; it's just wordier. Although E is technically not wrong, it is wordy as well, making C a better choice.

Sentence fragments

A sentence fragment is a sentence that isn't complete. In order to be complete, a sentence must be a complete thought with a subject and a verb. Beware of sentences that start with subordinating conjunctions (like *if, because, since,* and *although*). A clause that starts with a subordinating conjunction is dependent and cannot stand alone as a sentence, so be sure that you have another clause—an independent one—following the dependent one.

Try this question:

<u>Although now I can say I'm special and mean it.</u>

    A. Although now I can say I'm special and mean it.
    B. Although, now I can say I'm special and mean it.
    C. Although I called myself special before, now I really mean it.
    D. However I called myself before, now I can call myself special.
    E. Now I call myself special, however I didn't mean it before.

The **correct answer is C**. It consists of a dependent clause (*Although I called myself special before*) and an independent clause (*now I really mean it*). Choice A consists of a dependent clause only. So does choice B. The comma after *although* doesn't change that fact. Choice D is awkward, and choice E is a comma splice.

Wordiness

Clear, effective writing says more with fewer words. Inexperienced writers sometimes think that they need to add extra words to their papers to make them sound better. Instead, your goal should be to add more content (information, examples, description, explanation, etc.) instead of to add empty words. When in doubt on the "sentence improvement" section, choose the shorter answer. Although you won't be correct every time, you will be more often than not.

Try this question:

This is an excellent book that is extremely fun and helpful to read.

> A. This is an excellent book that is extremely fun and helpful
> B. This is an excellent book which is extremely fun and helpful
> C. This excellent book, which is extremely fun and helpful
> D. This book, which is helpful, is extremely fun
> E. This helpful book is extremely fun

The **correct answer is E** because it is short and sweet. A, B, and D all contain unnecessary words. Choice C makes the sentence into a fragment.

Word choice (Diction)

Sometimes you will have to identify words that are misused rather than grammatically incorrect. For example, a sentence may use the word *imply* where it should use *infer*. Here is a brief list of commonly confused words. Many more are available in grammar texts and online.

> accept (verb): to agree or take something offered
> except (preposition): excluding
>
> disinterested (adjective): impartial
> uninterested (adjective): not interested
>
> imply (verb): to indirectly suggest meaning
> infer (verb): to draw a conclusion
>
> disperse (verb): to scatter
> disburse (verb): to pay out
>
> than (conjunction): used for comparison
> then (adverb): next
>
> farther (adjective): more distant; more advanced
> further (adjective): in addition; extending beyond a certain point
>
> affect (verb): to produce an effect or change
> effect (noun): a result
>
> who (pronoun): referring to a person or to people
> which (pronoun): referring to a singular or plural thing
> that (pronoun): referring to things or a group of people
>
> conscience (noun): sense of right and wrong
> conscious (adjective): awake; aware

Identify the error in the sentence below:

<u>Their</u> <u>were</u> <u>too</u> many players on the field, so the referee called a <u>foul</u>. <u>no error</u>
  a   b   c   d   e

The **correct answer is A**. In this sentence, we need *there* rather than *their*.

Double negatives

In math, two negatives make a positive. The same is true in writing. If we use two negatives, they cancel each other out. For example, consider the sentence "I don't have **no** marbles." If I don't have no marbles, then I must have **some** marbles! When you want to make a negative statement, you should use only one negative word. Common negative words include *nothing, none, never, not, neither, scarcely, barely, hardly*, and *without*.

Identify the error in the sentence below:

I couldn't <u>never</u> <u>have finished</u> <u>that difficult</u> job by <u>myself</u>. <u>no error</u>
             a   b   c   d   e

The **correct answer is A**. Since the sentence already utilizes a negative word (*couldn't*), you don't need the second one (*never*). *Never* can be replaced with *ever* or removed altogether.

Idioms

An idiom is a word or expression that cannot be taken literally. For example, "He p*ulled the wool over my eyes*." Unfortunately (or perhaps fortunately!), there are no rules to learn about idioms. They either sound right, or they don't. The most common idiom errors you'll come across, though, are preposition errors. For example, it would be incorrect to say, "He pulled the wool *across* my eyes."

Identify the error in the sentence below:

<u>If</u> you keep <u>practicing</u> the oboe, you'll <u>eventually</u> get the <u>hang for it</u>. <u>no error</u>
a   b   c   d   e

The **correct answer is D**. The correct way to write the idiom is "hang *of* it."

Paragraph Improvement

A final type of multiple-choice question you will see in the writing section of the *SAT* is the "paragraph improvement" question. Here, you'll be asked to identify sentences that are out of order, should be rewritten or combined with other sentences, or should be removed from the paragraph altogether. You'll also be asked to select appropriate introductory and concluding sentences, transitional words, and supporting examples.

Try this practice question:

We visited a local animal shelter on Saturday. We wanted to pick out a new dog. As we walked through the corridor, each dog had its own way of sharing something about its personality. Some dogs barked, others jumped up and down, and still others cowered in the corners of their cages. We visited with several different dogs, but the one who stole our hearts was Bogart. This big, black dog with droopy ears and a wagging tail is now the newest member of our family.

What is the best way to combine the first two sentences of this paragraph?

   A. We visited a local animal shelter on Saturday, we wanted to pick out a new dog.
   B. We visited a local animal shelter on Saturday because we were hoping we would be able to pick out a new dog.
   C. Visiting a local animal shelter on Saturday, we were wanting to pick out a new dog.
   D. We visited a local animal shelter on Saturday to pick out a new dog.
   E. So that we could pick out a new dog, we went and visited a local animal shelter on Saturday.

The **correct answer is D** because it combines the two sentences without being wordy. Choice A, although not wordy, is a comma splice.

More Writing Practice Questions

1. Knocking over the <u>trashcan, debris flew everywhere</u>.

   A. trashcan, debris flew everywhere
   B. trashcan I caused debris to fly everywhere
   C. trashcan caused debris to fly everywhere
   D. trashcan is what caused the debris to fly everywhere
   E. trashcan resulted in the fact that debris flew everywhere

2. Jacob <u>and I</u> <u>only saw</u> one butterfly <u>in the garden</u> <u>yesterday</u>. <u>no error</u>
         a   b   c   d   e

3. <u>Working all the time and not having</u> time to practice baseball.

   A. Working all the time and not having
   B. Working all the time causes me not to have
   C. Because I work all the time, I don't have
   D. I work all the time therefore I don't have
   E. I work all the time and that means I don't have

4. This information goes along with the <u>topics that we have already touched base on</u>.

    A. topics that we have already touched base on
    B. topics that we have already addressed
    C. topics because we have already touched base on them
    D. topics on which we have already touched base
    E. topics, which we have already touched base on

5. Each of my friends <u>has</u> worked <u>hard</u> to make <u>this project</u> <u>successful</u>. <u>no error</u>
                       a   b   c   d   e

6. <u>Those students</u> have not had the training <u>they</u> need <u>to learn</u> to be <u>a safe driver</u>. <u>no error</u>
     a   b   c   d   e

7. <u>Over</u> the <u>course</u> of this week, we <u>hiked</u>, camped, and <u>went skiing</u>. <u>no error</u>
    a   b   c   d   e

8. The teacher caught Geoffrey <u>cheating, and he was kicked</u> out of class.

    A. cheating, and he was kicked
    B. cheating, and therefore he was kicked
    C. cheating and kicked him
    D. cheating after which he kicked him
    E. cheating, so he was kicked

9. I <u>can't make heads and tails of</u> this chemistry assignment.

    A. can't make heads and tails of
    B. can't make neither heads nor tails of
    C. can't make heads and tails about
    D. can't make heads or tails of
    E. can't hardly make heads or tails regarding

10. Hannah Williams is <u>the type</u> <u>of student</u> <u>whom</u> I admire <u>greatly</u>. <u>no error</u>
                                a   b   c   d   e

11. We <u>don't hardly</u> <u>have</u> <u>enough</u> time <u>to finish</u> our homework. <u>no error</u>
            a   b   c   d   e

12. I <u>used to</u> <u>dislike</u> all <u>types</u> of vegetables <u>accept</u> green beans. <u>no error</u>
     a   b   c   d   e

13. Which sentence should be removed from the following paragraph?

(1) Every year my family goes to the beach for a week in July. (2) We have stayed in the same beach house now for thirteen years. (3) The house has four bedrooms. (4) It has a large back porch. (5) We like to watch the boats and the sunsets from the porch. (6) There is always lots to do while we're at the beach, but we also find plenty of time to relax. (7) Sometimes I think it would be nice to visit the mountains for a change. (8) At the end of each beach trip, we feel rested and rejuvenated; and we look forward to the next year's visit.

    A. sentence #3
    B. sentence #4
    C. sentence #5
    D. sentence #6
    E. sentence #7

14. How could sentences 3, 4, and 5 best be combined?

    A. The house has four bedrooms and a large back porch from which we like to watch the boats and the sunsets.
    B. The house has four bedrooms, and it also has a large back porch that we like to watch the boats and the sunsets from.
    C. The house, which has four bedrooms and a large back porch, is great for watching the boats and the sunsets.
    D. Having four bedrooms, the house also has a large back porch, and we like to watch the boats and the sunsets from there.
    E. The house has four bedrooms, it also has a large back porch where we like to watch the boats and the sunsets.

Answers to Writing Practice Questions:

1. **C.** In the original sentence, *knocking over the trashcan* modifies *debris*. Choice B would work if it had a comma after the introductory phrase. Choices D and E are unnecessarily wordy.

2. **B.** *Only* should precede the word *one*. I saw *only one*. I didn't *only see* it.

3. **C.** The original sentence is a fragment. Choice D is a run-on. Choices B and E are unnecessarily wordy. Choice C is a complete–and concise–sentence.

4. **B.** Avoid wordiness! All of the other choices are awkward and wordy. Remember, shorter answers are usually better answers to the "sentence improvement" questions.

5. **E.** If you chose A, look again. *Each* is a singular pronoun; therefore, *has* is correct.

6. **D.** Multiple students can't be (one) *safe driver*. They must be *safe drivers*.

7. **D.** In order to make this sentence parallel in structure, we should say *hiked, camped, and skied*.

8. **C.** Although the sentence is not grammatically incorrect as it is, it does use passive voice. Choices B and E also contain passive voice. Choice D is wordy. Choice C uses active voice and is concise.

9. **D.** The idiom is *heads or tails*, which eliminates choices A, B, and C. Choice E contains a double negative.

10. **E.** If you chose C, look again. Remember that *whom* is used for direct objects, objects of prepositions, and indirect objects. In this case, *whom* is the direct object of *I admire*.

11. **A.** *Don't hardly* is a double negative. We can say either *don't have* or *hardly have*.

12. **D.** *Accept* is a verb. In this sentence we need to use *except*.

13. **E.** Sentence #7 is irrelevant to the rest of the paragraph because it introduces a new idea.

14. **A.** It is simply the least awkward sentence. It's also not wordy (like B and D), and it's not a comma splice (like E). Although C is not a bad choice, it is not as clear as A.

The Essay

Teaching students to write an essay is not the purpose of this guide. Instead, we will devote the remainder of this chapter to discussion about the criteria for scoring 6 on the essay. This information, taken directly from the *College Board* website, combined with the skill review provided above, should go a long way in helping you do well on the writing section of the *SAT Reasoning Test*.

At www.collegeboard.com, we learn the following about how the essay is scored:

"...Scoring Guide

The essay will be scored by experienced and trained high school and college teachers. Each essay will be scored by two people who won't know each other's scoring. They won't know the student's identity or school either. Each reader will give the essay a score from 1 to 6 (6 is the highest score) based on the following scoring guide.

SCORE OF 6
An essay in this category demonstrates *clear and consistent mastery*, although it may have a few minor errors. A typical essay

- effectively and insightfully develops a point of view on the issue and demonstrates outstanding critical thinking, using clearly appropriate examples, reasons, and other evidence to support its position
- is well organized and clearly focused, demonstrating clear coherence and smooth progression of ideas
- exhibits skillful use of language, using a varied, accurate, and apt vocabulary
- demonstrates meaningful variety in sentence structure
- is free of most errors in grammar, usage, and mechanics

SCORE OF 5
An essay in this category demonstrates *reasonably consistent mastery*, although it will have occasional errors or lapses in quality. A typical essay

- effectively develops a point of view on the issue and demonstrates strong critical thinking, generally using appropriate examples, reasons, and other evidence to support its position
- is well organized and focused, demonstrating coherence and progression of ideas
- exhibits facility in the use of language, using appropriate vocabulary demonstrates variety in sentence structure
- is generally free of most errors in grammar, usage, and mechanics

SCORE OF 4
An essay in this category demonstrates *adequate mastery*, although it will have lapses in quality. A typical essay

- develops a point of view on the issue and demonstrates competent critical thinking, using adequate examples, reasons, and other evidence to support its position
- is generally organized and focused, demonstrating some coherence and progression of ideas
- exhibits adequate but inconsistent facility in the use of language, using generally appropriate vocabulary
- demonstrates some variety in sentence structure
- has some errors in grammar, usage, and mechanics

SCORE OF 3

An essay in this category demonstrates *developing mastery* and is marked by ONE OR MORE of the following weaknesses:

- develops a point of view on the issue, demonstrating some critical thinking, but may do so inconsistently or use inadequate examples, reasons, or other evidence to support its position
- is limited in its organization or focus, or may demonstrate some lapses in coherence or progression of ideas
- displays developing facility in the use of language, but sometimes uses weak vocabulary or inappropriate word choice
- lacks variety or demonstrates problems in sentence structure
- contains an accumulation of errors in grammar, usage, and mechanics

SCORE OF 2

An essay in this category demonstrates *little mastery* and is flawed by ONE OR MORE of the following weaknesses:

- develops a point of view on the issue that is vague or seriously limited and demonstrates weak critical thinking, providing inappropriate or insufficient examples, reasons, or other evidence to support its position
- is poorly organized and/or focused, or demonstrates serious problems with coherence or progression of ideas
- displays very little facility in the use of language, using very limited vocabulary or incorrect word choice
- demonstrates frequent problems in sentence structure
- contains errors in grammar, usage, and mechanics so serious that meaning is somewhat obscured

SCORE OF 1

An essay in this category demonstrates *very little or no mastery* and is severely flawed by ONE OR MORE of the following weaknesses:

- develops no viable point of view on the issue, or provides little or no evidence to support its position
- is disorganized or unfocused, resulting in a disjointed or incoherent essay
- displays fundamental errors in vocabulary

- demonstrates severe flaws in sentence structure
- contains pervasive errors in grammar, usage, or mechanics that persistently interfere with meaning

Essays not written on the essay assignment will receive a score of zero…" [1]

We suggest that you review this chapter several times, until you feel confident that you understand the concepts addressed in the verbal section of the *SAT Reasoning Test*. Once you feel good about your skill review, tackle the CD game again.

By the way… How close are you to finding the virus that threatens the U.S. banking system in *Zero Hour Threat*? Hang in there. We are counting on you to do it!!

---

[1] *http://collegeboard.com/student/testing/sat/about/sat/essay_scoring.html*

Chapter Four: Math Skills Review

This chapter will cover most of the mathematics topics you will encounter on the *SAT* and offer advice to guide your test preparation. The first step begins with you. So many students approach this section of the test with an unhealthy amount of fear or anxiety. Familiarizing yourself with the format of the *SAT* math questions and becoming comfortable working with the equations that you will need to answer the questions will help you overcome this. Approaching this part of the test with a positive attitude and a plan of attack will help you achieve your desired score.

The mathematical reasoning sections of the *SAT* are designed to test your problem-solving abilities in topics that are generally covered in the math classes taken by most high school students. These topics include pre-algebra, algebra, and geometry. Although you will be tested on your knowledge of these subjects, it is your ability to apply what you have learned that will determine your success on the test.

Many of the formulas that you will need are provided for you on the test. You are being tested on your ability to apply these formulas when needed to arrive at the correct answers. Therefore, memorizing the formulas and their corresponding equations is not enough. Your comfort in applying your knowledge of what they mean is vital to success in solving mathematical problems on the test.

Thy Days Are Numbered: Properties of Numbers

A finite number of days remain before you are going to take the *SAT*, and it is always a good idea to begin preparing well in advance. Remember, you have been preparing for this day for several years now. This is where all of those hours spent in math classes finally pay off.

For the majority of the mathematical reasoning questions, obtaining the correct answer will depend on your ability to manipulate numerical values. Approximately eighty percent (80%) of your answers will be a numerical value. In this section, you will review the types of numbers that may be encountered and some of their basic properties.

Classes and Types of Numbers

Yes, numbers do come in different types! We will begin by covering some of the basic terminology used to describe the different classes or types of numbers.

- **Counting Numbers**
  The **counting numbers**, also referred to as the **natural numbers**, are probably the first numbers you ever encountered in life. Beginning with 1, they continue infinitely in the positive direction.
  Examples: 1, 2, 3, 4, 5, ...

- **Integer**

  The integers, also referred to as **whole numbers**, are the counting numbers together with their negatives (and zero). They continue infinitely in both the negative and positive directions.

  Examples: ..., -4, -3, -2, -1, 0, 1, 2, 3, 4, ...

- **Decimal**

  The decimal system allows us to write numbers that are arbitrarily small. We can represent **numbers or parts of a number that are less than 1** by **using a decimal**. The place values to the left of the decimal represent tenths, hundredths, thousandths, and so on.

  Examples: 1.2, 1.003, 0.00234, and 1.235

- **Rational Numbers**

  Rational numbers can be written as a **ratio or fraction involving two integers.** Any number that can be written as a terminating or a repeating decimal is a rational number.

  Examples: $1/2$, 0.033, and 2

- **Irrational Numbers**

  Irrational numbers consist of any real numbers that are not rational numbers; that is, they cannot be written as a ratio of two integers.

  Examples: $\sqrt{2}$, $\sqrt{3}$, and π

- **Real Numbers**

  The real numbers consist of **all rational and irrational numbers.**

- **Negative, Positive, or Not**

  This is included here because you will often encounter this terminology when describing classes of numbers.

  - A **negative number** is **any number that is less than zero.**
    - -1, $-\sqrt{2}$, and $-1/33$ are negative numbers.
  - A positive number is any number greater than zero.
    - 2, $\sqrt{3}$, and 34/53 are positive numbers.
  - **Zero** is **neither negative nor positive.**
  - **We cannot classify imaginary or complex numbers as positive or negative**, although **we can classify the real or the imaginary component.**
    - $3-2i$ is neither positive nor negative, although the real component (3) is positive and the imaginary component (-2) is negative.
  - **Non-negative numbers include zero and all positive numbers.**
    - 0, 3, and $\sqrt{5}$ are examples.
  - **Non-positive numbers include zero and all negative numbers.**
    - 0, $-\pi$, and -1/28 are examples.

Multiples, Factors, and Primes

A *multiple* of a number is any product of that number and an integer. So, 4, 8, 12, 16, and 20 are multiples of 4 because 4 x 1 = 4, 4 x 2 = 8, 4 x 3 = 12, 4 x 4 = 16, and 4 x 5 = 20. The test writers are typically going to consider the positive multiples of a number. They may even refer to the positive multiples as simply the multiples. However, multiples of a number can be negative as well. Note that –4, –8, –12, –16, and –20 are also multiples of 4. Multiples of a number need not be positive or negative. Although the chances it will come up on the test may be small, it certainly doesn't hurt to know that zero is a multiple of every number, since zero is an integer and any number x0 = 0. The lowest (positive) multiple shared by two numbers is called the *least common multiple*. The multiples of 3 and 8 are shown below:

Multiples of 3: 3, 6, 9, 12, 15, 18, 21, 24, 27, 30, 33, …
Multiples of 8: 8, 16, 24, 32, 40, 48, 56, 64, 72, 80, 88, …

As you can see, the first multiple to appear in both lists is 24. Therefore, 24 is the least common multiple of 3 and 8.

A *factor* of a number is any (positive) integer that evenly divides (remainder of 0) into the number. The number 18 has factors of 2, 3, 6, and 9 because 18 / 9 = 2, 18 / 6 = 3, 18 / 3 = 6, and 18 / 2 = 9. Any given number is a multiple of all its factors. The term ***greatest common factor*** is given to **the largest factor shared by two numbers**. The greatest common factor of 21 and 28 is 7, since 7 is the largest number that is a factor of both numbers. Although it is unlikely that you will simply be asked to factor a number for the test, being able to factor numbers will be important to answering many of the questions.

A *prime number* is any integer greater than 1 whose only factors (positive divisors) are 1 and itself. Three (3) is a prime number because the only factors of 3 are 1 and 3. Six (6) is not a prime number because the factors of 6 are 1, 2, 3, and 6. Although we won't get into why here, note that 1 is not considered a prime number. We can write every positive integer as a unique product of prime numbers. This is referred to as the *prime factorization* of a number. The number 4620 has a prime factorization of 2•2•3•5•7•11. The prime factorization of a number is unique; that is to say, there is no other combination of prime factors that will give the same product. This leads us to another concept that you may encounter, although probably not more than once on a given test. Two numbers are said to be *relatively prime* if they have no factors (other than 1) in common. The numbers 198 = 2•3•3•11, and 455 = 5•7•13, are relatively prime because they share no common factors in their prime factorization.

When completely factoring a number, begin by removing any obvious factors such as 2, 5, and 10. This will make it easier to examine any of the less obvious factors. In factoring a number, the following divisibility rules will be helpful.

1. One (1) is a factor of any whole number.

2. Any even number (ends in 0, 2, 4, 6, or 8) will be divisible by 2.
    • 312, 233, 247, 256 is divisible by 2, while 246, 468, 324, 221 is not.

3. Add up the digits in the number. If the sum of the digits is divisible by 3, then the number is divisible by 3 as well. Note that you can do this recursively for large numbers.
   - How would you determine if the number 937, 689, 865, 863 is divisible by 3? Add up the digits: $9 + 3 + 7 + 6 + 8 + 9 + 8 + 6 + 5 + 8 + 6 + 3 = 78$. Is 78 divisible by 3? $7 + 8 = 15$ and $15 \div 3 = 5$ so the original number is divisible by 3.

4. If the last two digits are divisible by 4, then the number is divisible by 4.
   - 432, 235, 916 is divisible by 4 because 16 is divisible by 4.

5. Any number ending in 0 or 5 is divisible by 5.

6. Any even number that is divisible by 3 will be divisible by 6.
   (This is just the combination of rules 2 and 3 above.)
   - 14 is divisible by 2 (because it ends in 4) but not by 3.
     (1+4=5, which is not divisible by 3), so 14 is not divisible by 6.
   - 15 is divisible by 3 ($1 + 5 = 6$, which is divisible by 3) but not by 2 (because it ends in 5), so 15 is not divisible by 6.
   - 18 is divisible by 2 (because it ends in 8) and by 3 (because $1 + 8 = 9$, which is divisible by 3), so 18 is divisible by 6.

7. Double the last digit and subtract the results from the remaining digits. If this number is divisible by 7, then the original number is also divisible by 7. This can be done recursively as well.
   - To determine if 19,565 is divisible by 7, do the following:
     $$\begin{array}{r} 1956 \ (5 \times 2 = 10) \\ - \ 10 \\ \hline 194 \ (6 \times 2 = 12) \\ - \ 12 \\ \hline 18 \ (2 \times 2 = 4) \\ - \ 4 \\ \hline 14 / 7 = 2 \end{array}$$

8. If the last three digits are divisible by 8, then the entire number is divisible by 8. This rule isn't as helpful as some of the others. You can also just look for successive factors of 2 (remember that $2 \cdot 2 \cdot 2 = 8$).
   - The number 257,392,104 is divisible by 8 because 104 is divisible by 8. Also, note that 257,392,104/2 = 128,696,052, 128,696,052/2 = 64,348,026, and 64,348,026/2 = 32,174,013.

9. This rule is similar to rule 3 above. If the sum of the digits is divisible by 9, then the number is divisible by 9.
   - 423,421,264,413 is divisible by 9 because the sum of the digits is $36 = (9 \times 4)$.

10. Any number ending in 0 is divisible by 10.

Properties of Numbers Practice Problems

1. True or false: All natural numbers are non-negative.
    A) True
    B) False

2. Which of the following are positive integers?
    I. 2
    II. 1/3
    III. 0
    IV. −3
    V. π

    A) I, II, III, and IV
    B) I, II, and III
    C) I and III
    D) I only
    E) II only

3. True or false: All non-negative integers are natural numbers.
    A) True
    B) False

4. Which of the following are non-positive rational numbers?
    I. −1
    II. 0
    III. $-\sqrt{2}$
    IV. $-\sqrt{4}$
    V. 1/3

    A) I, II, III, and IV
    B) I, II, and IV
    C) I, II, and V
    D) I, III, and IV
    E) I and V

5. What is 1/500 written as a decimal?
    A) 0.01
    B) 0.02
    C) 0.05
    D) 0.002
    E) 0.005

6. Which of the following are multiples of 8?
   - I. 24
   - II. 36
   - III. 4
   - IV. 1,624
   - V. 3,001

   A) I, II, and III
   B) I, II, and IV
   C) I and IV
   D) II and IV
   E) I and V

7. The least common multiple of 10 and 18 is
   A) 2.
   B) 80.
   C) 90.
   D) 180.
   E) 360.

8. Which of the following is not a factor of 20,790?
   A) 2
   B) 3
   C) 6
   D) 11
   E) 20

9. The greatest common factor of 874 and 1,995 is
   A) 3.
   B) 7.
   C) 15.
   D) 19.
   E) 23.

10. The correct prime factorization of 22,770 is
    A) 6 • 5 • 11 • 23.
    B) 2 • 3 • 5 • 11 • 23.
    C) 2 • 3 • 3 • 5 • 11 • 23.
    D) 2 • 3 • 3 • 3 • 5 • 7 • 11.
    E) 3 • 3 • 5 • 5 • 5 • 7 • 7.

11. Of the following pairs of numbers, which pair is mutually prime?
   A) 43,010 and 150,423
   B) 3,705 and 7,116
   C) 99,009 and 144,177,345
   D) 68 and 13,247,352,132
   E) 22 and 319,209,649

Note: Answers may be found on page 108.

Frustrations with Fractions

If fractions get you frustrated, you are not alone. Many students are uncomfortable working with fractions. **A fraction is used to describe a part of a whole. The numerator (top) describes the part, and the denominator (bottom) describes the whole.** In the fraction 2/3, the numerator is 2 and the denominator is 3. We'll discuss operations such as addition and multiplication in a later section. For now, we just want you to familiarize yourself with the concepts of equivalent fractions, reducing fractions, and common denominators.

Equivalent Fractions

Stated simply, **two fractions that describe the same part of the whole are considered** *equivalent fractions.* If two friends cut a pie in half, they can each take 1/2 of the whole. What if they both cut their piece of the pie into two pieces? They now each have two pieces of the pie, which is now in four pieces. So, they each have 2/4 of the pie. 2/4 and 1/2 are equivalent fractions. In fact, 362/724 and 1/2 are equivalent fractions. Two equivalent fractions will be the same when completely reduced (written in simplest form). Both 2/4 and 362/724 simplify to 1/2. When one or both of the fractions contain large numbers, it may not be in your best interest to try to reduce or simplify them, although you could certainly do this. We can compare two fractions by simply cross multiplying. For example, if we are asked to compare $^{1,728}/_{4,032}$ and $^{3,972}/_{9,268}$ we probably don't want to simplify these fractions. We will want to cross multiply.

$$(1{,}728 \times 9{,}268 = 16{,}015{,}104) \; \frac{1{,}728}{4{,}032} \times \frac{3{,}972}{9{,}268} \; (4{,}032 \times 3{,}972 = 16{,}015{,}104)$$

Because the cross products are the same, the fractions are equivalent. Had the product on the left been larger, the fraction to the left would be the larger of the two. Similarly, had the product on the right been larger, the fraction to the right would be the larger of the two. For example, $^{74}/_{100} < ^{3}/_{4} < ^{76}/_{100}$.

$$(74 \times 4 = 296) \; \frac{74}{100} \times \frac{3}{4} \; (100 \times 3 = 300)$$

$$(3 \times 100 = 300) \; \frac{3}{4} \times \frac{76}{100} \; (4 \times 76 = 304)$$

Reducing Fractions

Reducing and simplifying fractions will require you to be able to identify the common factors between the numerator and the denominator. This is where the divisibility rules will come into play. You will be looking for factors that can divide both the numerator and the denominator. You can do this either by writing out the prime factorization of both the numerator and the denominator or just by examination. Consider the problem of simplifying the fraction $420/630$. You could simply write out the prime factorization of 420 and 630, canceling any common factors. After some work you would arrive at the correct answer.

$$\frac{420}{630} = \frac{\cancel{2} \times 2 \times \cancel{3} \times \cancel{5} \times \cancel{7}}{\cancel{2} \times 2 \times \cancel{3} \times \cancel{5} \times \cancel{7}} = \frac{2}{3}$$

A second, and often quicker, approach will be simply to look for common factors by inspection. We can easily see that both 420 and 630 are divisible by 10. This leaves us with $42/63$. Both 42 and 63 are divisible by 3 (the sums of the digits are 6 and 9, respectively), so we are left with $14/21$. Removing the final common factor of 7 will leave the correct answer of $2/3$.

You will probably encounter one or more *improper fractions* on the test. An improper fraction is one that represents a whole number. Answers for the multiple-choice questions will typically be written as *mixed numbers*. Mixed numbers represent an improper fraction as a whole number and a fractional component. For example, 7/3 is an improper fraction. Three (3) divides into 7 twice with a remainder of 1. We could thus write 7/3 as the mixed number $2\frac{1}{3}$. You will also encounter the situation where you will have to convert a mixed number to an improper fraction, especially when multiplying or dividing with fractions. To do this, simply multiply the whole number by the denominator, add the result to the numerator, and divide the sum by the denominator. Using our previous example, writing $2\frac{1}{3}$ as an improper fraction would look something like

$$2\frac{1}{3} = \frac{(2 \times 3) + 1}{3} = \frac{6 + 1}{3} = \frac{7}{3}$$

Finding Common Denominators

The most common problem students encounter with fractions involves finding a common denominator, or more importantly, the *least common denominator*. Before you can add or subtract fractions, you will need to find a common denominator. Probably the simplest way to find a common denominator will be to take the product of the two denominators. For example, $2/3$ and $1/4$ can be written with a common denominator of.

$$\frac{2}{3} \times \frac{4}{4} = \frac{8}{12} \qquad \qquad \frac{1}{4} \times \frac{3}{3} = \frac{3}{12}$$

Although this can be done pretty quickly, it may result in answers requiring a significant amount of simplification. This is because the common denominator that results is not necessarily the *least* common denominator. To find the least common denominator will require a couple of steps. We begin by factoring both of the denominators. With this factorization in hand, we will take as the least common denominator the union of these two sets. We thus simply multiply the numerator and the denominator of each fraction by the missing factors to arrive at equivalent fractions with the least common denominator as the denominator. Consider the fractions $^{91}/_{660}$ and $^{37}/_{42}$. Begin by factoring both denominators:

$$\underset{2\bullet 2\bullet 3\bullet 5\bullet 11}{\frac{91}{660}} \qquad \underset{2\bullet 3\bullet 5\bullet 7}{\frac{53}{210}}$$

The least common denominator will thus be 2•2•3•5•7•11=4,620. All we need to do now is multiply the numerator and denominator of each fraction by the missing factors.

$$\underset{2\bullet 2\bullet 3\bullet 5\bullet 11}{\frac{91}{660}} \times \frac{7}{7} = \frac{637}{4,620} \qquad \underset{2\bullet 3\bullet 5\bullet 7}{\frac{53}{210}} \times \frac{2\bullet 11}{2\bullet 11} = \frac{1,166}{4,620}$$

It may not be obvious since we still have fractions with rather large numbers, but this really did make things simpler. Had we simply multiplied the two denominators together, we would have gotten a common denominator of 138,600.

Fractions Practice Problems

1. In which of the following fractions are both numbers a multiple of 8?

    I. $\dfrac{49{,}428}{86{,}500}$ IV. $\dfrac{47{,}325}{34{,}321}$

    II. $\dfrac{9{,}460}{16{,}555}$ V. $\dfrac{36}{63}$

    III. $\dfrac{12{,}357}{31{,}367}$

    A) I, II, III, and V.
    B) I, II, and V.
    C) I and II.
    D) I and V.
    E) II and V.

2. Which of the following are greater than $5/11$?

    I. 1/2   IV. 34/77
    II. 65/132   V. 40/87
    III. 17/33

    A) I, II, III, and V.
    B) I, II, and III.
    C) I, II, and V.
    D) I and II.
    E) I and V.

3. The fraction 720/780 is equivalent to which of the following?
    A) 5/6
    B) 3/4
    C) 6/7
    D) 12/13
    E) 13/17

4. Write $9{,}702/6{,}930$ as a mixed number in simplest form.
    A) 7/5
    B) $1\frac{2}{3}$
    C) $1\frac{2}{5}$
    D) 5/3
    E) $1\frac{29}{75}$

5. Write $5^{12}/_{13}$ as an improper fraction.
   A) $^{72}/_{13}$
   B) $^{65}/_{13}$
   C) $^{17}/_{13}$
   D) $^{60}/_{13}$
   E) $^{77}/_{13}$

6. What is the least common denominator of $^{7}/_{12}$ and $^{23}/_{26}$?
   A) $^{7}/_{156}$
   B) $^{1}/_{156}$
   C) 156
   D) 24
   E) 312

Note: Answers may be found on Page 113.

We're Going to Have to Operate: Operations with Numbers

This subtitle may sound like a really bad joke. OK, maybe it is, but many of the common mistakes made by students on the *SAT* math tests are due to simple mistakes in operations: addition, subtraction, multiplication, and division. More often than not, this is the result of rushing through an otherwise easy problem and arriving at one of the wrong answers. The test writers know what mistakes students commonly make, and they use this information when coming up with the wrong answer choices. This is where the "easy" problems get you. **Remember to take your time so you won't miss these questions!**

Also, **remember the all-important *order of operations*.** (We'll review this as well.) Just as for a surgeon, the order in which you do things when performing mathematical operations is vitally important. We'll review some of the basics of addition, subtraction, multiplication, and division here. If you feel that you need more help or practice with any of these, consult your math teacher. Your ability to perform basic mathematical operations will be extremely important to your success on the test. You will be able to use your calculator on this part of the test, but your understanding of the basic mathematical operations will help prevent careless mistakes. Also, some of the more advanced calculators are capable of performing many of the more advanced operations as well, such as multiplying and dividing complex numbers. Consult the manual for your calculator to find out what its capabilities are.

Addition

When adding two (or more) numbers together, the numbers to be added are called *addends* and the answer is the *sum*. So, in the problem below, 3,432 and 291 are the addends and 3,723 is the sum.

$$\begin{array}{cccc} \overset{1}{3{,}432} & \overset{1}{3{,}432} & \overset{1}{3{,}432} & \overset{1}{3{,}432} \\ +\,291 & +\,291 & +\,291 & +\,291 \\ \hline 3 & 23 & 723 & 3{,}723 \end{array}$$

When adding integers, always be careful to keep the columns straight and line everything up with the units column. Addition is *commutative*. This means that the order in which we add the numbers does not change the final answer. Don't let this confuse you. It's something you already know: $2 + 3 = 3 + 2 = 5$. Also, addition is *associative*. This means that we can group the numbers in any manner we choose and still get the same answer. For example $(3 + 2) + 4 = 5 + 4 = 9 = 3 + 6 = 3 + (2 + 4)$. Although this is not meant to be thorough enough to teach you addition, we'll look at a few things you need to remember. Most of this should already be familiar to you.

- When adding integer numbers, remember the following:
   Even + Even = Even (2 + 4 = 6)
   Odd + Odd = Even (3 + 3 = 6)
   Even + Odd = Odd (2 + 3 = 5)

- When adding negative and positive numbers, you may find it advantageous to rewrite the problem as a subtraction problem.

  $$234 + 137 + -295 = (234 + 137) - 295 = 371 - 295 = 76$$

- When adding decimal numbers, always align the columns on the decimal point. The proper place for the decimal point in the final answer will be directly beneath the decimal points in the problem.

$$\begin{array}{r} \overset{1}{1.324} \\ + \; 2.190 \\ \hline \mathbf{3.514} \end{array}$$

- When adding fractions, always find a *common denominator*. There are many different ways that you can do this. Deciding which way is best really depends on what works best for you. Consider the problem $\frac{5}{12} + \frac{3}{10}$.

You could first proceed by multiplying both the numerator and the denominator of each addend by the denominator of the other addend.

$$\frac{5}{12} \times \left(\frac{10}{10}\right) + \frac{3}{10} \times \left(\frac{12}{12}\right) = \frac{50}{120} + \frac{36}{120} = \frac{86}{120}$$

Now, you need to simplify the answer. We can pull out a common factor of 2.

$$\frac{86/2}{120/2} = \frac{43}{60}$$

Remember, as long as we do the same thing to both the numerator and the denominator, we have not changed the fraction; for example, 86/120 and 43/60 are *equivalent fractions*.

Going back to the original problem, we could have also found a common denominator by factoring the denominator of each addend and taking, as our *common denominator*, the union of all factors. This should give us what is known as the *least common denominator*.

$$\frac{5}{12} + \frac{3}{10} = \frac{5}{2 \cdot 2 \cdot 3} + \frac{3}{2 \cdot 5}$$

Our common denominator will thus have two factors of 2, one 3, and one 5. We can then multiply the numerator and denominator of each addend by the necessary factors.

$$\frac{5}{12} \times (\frac{5}{5}) + \frac{3}{10} \times (\frac{2 \cdot 3}{2 \cdot 3}) = \frac{25}{60} + \frac{18}{60} = \frac{43}{60}$$

This answer needs no further simplification.

- When adding fractions written as mixed numbers, you don't have to rewrite them as improper fractions. Add the integer components and then add the fractions. Remember that you will still have to find a common denominator, and you may have to simplify the fractional component of the result. Consider the problem,

$$11\frac{3}{4} + 12\frac{3}{5}$$

We will begin by adding the whole numbers and then adding the fractions, making sure to find a common denominator.

$$11\frac{3}{4} + 12\frac{3}{5} = (11+12) + (\frac{3}{4} + \frac{3}{5})$$

$$= 23 + (\frac{3}{4} (\times \frac{5}{5}) + \frac{3}{5} (\times \frac{4}{4}))$$

$$= 23 + (\frac{15}{20} + \frac{12}{20})$$

$$= 23 + \frac{27}{20}$$

Now we'll have to rewrite this answer in simplest form. 27/20 is an improper fraction. 20 goes into 27 once, with a remainder of 7; thus,

$$23 + \frac{27}{20} = 23 + 1\frac{7}{20} = 24\frac{7}{20}$$

Subtraction

When subtracting two numbers, **if** the number we are subtracting from is the *minuend*, and the result is called the *difference*. In the example problem below, 430 is the minuend, 220 the subtrahend, and 210 the difference.

$$\begin{array}{r} 430 \\ -\ 220 \\ \hline 210 \end{array}$$

Just like with addition, when subtracting integers always you should line everything up with the units column. Here are some more things you need to remember with subtraction. Again, get more help if you feel that you need it.

- When subtracting integer, remember the following:
    Even − Even = Even (6 − 4 = 2)
    Odd − Odd = Even (5 − 3 = 2)
    Even − Odd = Odd (8 − 5 = 3)
    Odd − Even = Odd (7 − 4 = 3)

- When subtracting a negative number from a positive number (or vice versa), you may find it advantageous to rewrite the problem as an addition problem.

    $$234 - (-137) = 234 + 137 = 371$$

- When subtracting decimal numbers, always align the columns on the decimal point. The proper place for the decimal point in the final answer will be directly beneath the decimal points in the problem. Also, remember that you may borrow from the units to the left if needed. This is demonstrated in the problem below.

$$\begin{array}{ccccc} 21.324 & 21.3\overset{2\ 12}{2}4 & 21.\overset{2\ 12}{3}24 & \overset{1\ 11\ 2\ 12}{21.324} & \overset{1\ 11\ 2\ 12}{21.324} \\ -2.190 & -2.190 & -2.190 & -\ 2.190 & -2.190 \\ \hline 4 & 34 & .134 & 9.134 & 19.134 \end{array}$$

- When subtracting fractions, always find a common denominator. Consider the problem below.

$$\frac{7}{12} - \frac{13}{30} = (\frac{7}{12} \times \frac{5}{5}) - (\frac{13}{30} \times \frac{2}{2})$$

$$= (\frac{35}{60} \times \frac{26}{60}) - (\frac{9}{60} \times \frac{3}{20})$$

- When subtracting fractions written as mixed numbers, you don't have to rewrite them as improper fractions. Subtract the integer components and then subtract the fractions. Remember that you will still have to find a common denominator, and you may have to simplify the fractional component of the result. Consider the problem,

$$12\frac{3}{5} - 11\frac{3}{4}$$

We will begin by subtracting the whole numbers and then subtract the fractions, making sure to find a common denominator.

$$27\frac{3}{5} - 11\frac{3}{4} = (27 - 11) + (\frac{3}{5} - \frac{3}{4})$$

$$= 16 + (\frac{3}{5} - \frac{3}{4})$$

Were 3/5 not less than 3/4, we could just go ahead and subtract the fractions and arrive at the answer. In this case, we will have to essentially borrow from the whole number.

$$16 + (\frac{3}{5} - \frac{3}{4}) = 15 + 1 + (\frac{3}{5} - \frac{3}{4})$$

$$= 15 + (\frac{8}{5} - \frac{3}{4})$$

$$= 15 + (\frac{32}{20} - \frac{15}{20}) = 15\frac{17}{20}$$

Multiplication

You will probably do much of the multiplication with your calculator. However, it is still a good idea to know what is going on. The answer to a multiplication problem is called the *product*. **Multiplication can be thought of as collective additions**. When we say 4 x 3 we could view this as either 4 + 4 + 4 or as 3 + 3 + 3 + 3; the answer is still 12. Multiplication is commutative, meaning that 4 x 3 = 3 x 4. Here are some things to remember with multiplication:

- When multiplying integer, remember the following:
    Even x Even = Even (2 x 4 = 8)
    Odd x Odd = Odd (3 x 5 = 15)
    Even x Odd = Odd (2 x 3 = 6)
    Odd x Even = Odd (3 x 2 = 6)

- When multiplying integers with more than one digit, you must keep up with the place value. When multiplying 127 and 34 we begin by multiplying by 4.

    ```
      1 2
      127
    x  34
    -----
      508
    ```

Now we multiply by 3, leaving a zero to the right because we are actually multiplying by 30.

    ```
       2
      127
    x  34
    -----
      508
     3810
    -----
     4318
    ```

- When multiplying positive and negative numbers, remember:
    Positive x Positive = Positive
    Negative x Negative = Positive
    Positive x Negative = Negative
    Negative x Positive = Negative

- When multiplying decimal, proceed just as if you are multiplying integers. The number of places to the right of the decimal point in the product is simply the sum of the number of places to the right of the decimal point in the numbers being multiplied. When we multiply 21.324 by 2.19, we will have 3 + 2 = 5 places to the right in the final answer.

    ```
     1 2 2 3       1 2 2 3       1 2 2 3       1 2 2 3
     21.324        21.324        21.324        21.324
    x  2.19       x  2.19       x  2.19       x  2.19
    -------       -------       -------       -------
     191916        191916        191916        191916
                   213240        213240        213240
                                4264800       4264800
                                              -------
                                              46.69956
    ```

- Multiplication with fractions is much simpler than addition and subtraction. You do not need to find a common denominator. Just multiply the numerators and then multiply the denominators. You may have to simplify afterwards.

$$\frac{3}{4} \times \frac{2}{3} = \frac{6}{12} = \frac{1}{2}$$

When multiplying a series of fractions, it helps to recognize factors that you can cancel prior to multiplication. In the problem below, we can cancel the 3 and the 5 because they appear in both the numerator and the denominator. We can even cancel the 2 in the numerator with a factor of 2 from the 4 in the denominator.

$$\frac{1}{3} \times \frac{\cancel{2}}{\cancel{5}} \times \frac{\cancel{3}}{\cancel{4}_2} \times \frac{\cancel{5}}{7} = \frac{1}{14}$$

By canceling these factors prior to multiplication, we arrive at an answer that is in reduced form. Had we not done this and just multiplied across, we would have had to reduce $^{30}/_{420}$.

- When multiplying fractions written as mixed numbers, rewrite them as improper fractions. Consider the problem,

$$3\frac{3}{5} \times 4\frac{3}{4}$$

We will begin by rewriting the mixed numbers as improper fractions and multiplying across.

$$3\frac{3}{5} \times 4\frac{3}{4} = \frac{\cancel{18}^9}{5} \times \frac{19}{\cancel{4}_2} = \frac{171}{10}$$

Division

Division is closely related to working with fractions. The number being divided (numerator) is called the *dividend*, and the number we are dividing by (denominator) is called the *divisor*. The answer is called the *quotient*. So, $6 \div 4 = ^6/_2 = ^3/_1$ where 6 is the dividend, 2 is the divisor, and 3 is the quotient. The divisor won't always divide evenly into the dividend (the quotient is not always a whole number). Four (4) goes into 6 once. The *remainder* is 2. This can also be expressed as $6 \div 4 = ^6/_4 = ^3/_2 = 1\ ^1/_2$. Four (4) goes into 6 one and a half times. We can thus always express the answer as a mixed number with the fractional component written as the remainder divided by the divisor ($^2/_4 = ^1/_2$ in the problem above).

- When dividing decimals, move the decimal point in the divisor all the way to the right and then in the dividend the same number of places.

$$2.34 \div 0.06 = 234 \div 6 = 39$$

- When dividing positive and negative numbers, remember:
  Positive ÷ Positive = Positive
  Negative ÷ Negative = Positive
  Positive ÷ Negative = Negative
  Negative ÷ Positive = Negative

- Division with fractions is much simpler than addition and subtraction. You can convert the problem into multiplication by flipping the divisor, and you do not need to find a common denominator.

$$\frac{3}{4} \div \frac{1}{2} = \frac{\frac{3}{4}}{\frac{1}{2}} = \frac{3}{4} \times \frac{2}{1} = \frac{6}{4} = \frac{3}{2} = 1\frac{1}{2}$$

- When dividing fractions written as mixed numbers, rewrite them as improper fractions:

$$4\frac{3}{4} \div 3\frac{1}{4} = \frac{19}{4} \div \frac{13}{4} = \frac{19}{4} \times \frac{4}{13} = \frac{19}{13} = 1\frac{6}{13}$$

Order of Operations

The order in which we apply operations is extremely important. Questions that test your knowledge of the correct order of operations frequently show up on the test. There is a simple pneumonic device, "PEMDAS," that will assist you in remembering the proper order. Students are often taught to remember this using the phrase "**P**lease **E**xcuse **M**y **D**ear **A**unt **S**ally," among others. The letters stand for

1. **P**arentheses
2. **E**xponents
3. **M**ultiplication and **D**ivision
4. **A**ddition and **S**ubtraction

Consider the problem $3(2^4 - 2 \cdot 3)^2 - 2 \cdot 3$. We begin by evaluating everything inside the parentheses, remembering the correct order of operations when doing so.

$$3(2^4 - 2 \cdot 3)^2 - 2 \cdot 3 = 3(16 - 2 \cdot 3)^2 - 2 \cdot 3$$

$$= 3(16 - 6)^2 - 2 \cdot 3$$

$$= 3(10)^2 - 2 \cdot 3$$

Now that we have evaluated everything inside the parentheses, we proceed to evaluate the exponents, followed by all multiplication and division, and then by all addition and subtraction.

$$3(10)^2 - 2 \cdot 3 = 3 \cdot 100 - 2 \cdot 3$$
$$= 300 - 6$$
$$= 294$$

Although the example has used integers, the rules concerning the order of operations should be applied for operations with any of the classes of numbers we have already discussed.

Operations Practice Problems

1) $\dfrac{187}{420} + \dfrac{91}{510} =$

    A) $\dfrac{278}{930}$ D) $\dfrac{133,580}{214,200}$

    B) $\dfrac{278}{420}$ E) $\dfrac{4,453}{7140}$

    C) $\dfrac{278}{510}$

2) $5\dfrac{1}{3} - 2\dfrac{3}{4} =$

    A) $3\dfrac{7}{12}$ D) $2\dfrac{1}{3}$

    B) $2\dfrac{7}{12}$ E) $3\dfrac{3}{4}$

    C) $3\dfrac{5}{12}$

3) 27.2347 − 13.395 =
    A) 14.1617   D) 14.8397
    B) 25.8952   E) 13.1617
    C) 13.8397

4) 3.257 x 0.749 =
    A) 2.430439   D) 0.2439493
    B) 24.39493   E) 2.439493
    C) 24.39493

5) What is the quotient of $5\,^3/_4$ divided by $2\,^2/_3$?

    A) $2\dfrac{8}{9}$ D) $\dfrac{23}{4}$

    B) $\dfrac{46}{3}$ E) $\dfrac{31}{7}$

    C) $2\dfrac{5}{32}$

6) Simplify $\dfrac{4^3 - (8.5 - 2 \cdot 1.25)^2}{3 + \dfrac{3}{4} + (1 + \dfrac{1}{2})^2 - 1}$

    A) 4   D) -7.4801571

    B) $\dfrac{112}{13}$ E) $4\dfrac{2}{3}$

    C) 2

7) $(6.31 - 2.4^2) \cdot 1.75 - 0.25 =$

    A) 26.504175   D) 22.93215

    B) 0.7125   E) 0.825

    C) 0.55

8) $\dfrac{4\dfrac{3}{4} - 2\dfrac{1}{4} + 1\dfrac{1}{3}}{3\dfrac{2}{3}} =$

    A) $\dfrac{147}{128}$ D) $1\dfrac{1}{4}$

    B) $\dfrac{45}{64}$ E) 5

    C) 2

Note: Answers may be found on Page 113.

What's With All the Letters: Algebraic Expressions and Manipulation

Many of the questions on the *SAT* math test may not include numbers at all. These questions (and others) will test your knowledge of basic algebraic concepts. You will need to be comfortable working with algebraic expressions and functions, solving for an unknown variable, factoring and simplifying algebraic expressions, and applying algebraic concepts to problem solving.

Definitions and Basics

An **algebraic expression** is a collection of terms combined by addition, subtraction, or both in which letters or variables are used to represent numbers. **Terms** are made up of numbers or variables combined by multiplication or division. In order to achieve success on the exam, you will need to be able to apply the basic operations of arithmetic to algebraic expressions.

For example, like terms can be combined:

$$4x + 5x = 9x$$
$$5a + 6b + 2a - 3b = 7a + 3b$$
$$15x - 3y - (-6y) + 7x - 5 = 22x + 3y - 5$$
$$(x - 5)(x + 2) = x^2 - 3x - 10$$
$$\frac{10ab}{2b} = 5a$$

Definitions for algebraic exponents

$$x^3 = x \cdot x \cdot x$$

$$a^{-4} = \frac{1}{a} \cdot \frac{1}{a} \cdot \frac{1}{a} \cdot \frac{1}{a} = \frac{1}{a^4}$$

$$x^0 = 1$$

$$x^{a/b} = \sqrt[b]{x^a} = (\sqrt[b]{x})^a$$

$$y^{1/2} = \sqrt{y}$$

Key concepts to remember:

- **Add exponents** when multiplying expressions with the same base:

$$x^3 \cdot x^4 = (x \cdot x \cdot x)(x \cdot x \cdot x \cdot x) = x^7$$
$$x^a + x^b = x^{a+b}$$

The same rule applies for negative exponents:

$$y^4 \cdot y^{-2} = (y \cdot y \cdot y \cdot y) \cdot (\tfrac{1}{y} \cdot \tfrac{1}{y}) = y^2$$

• **Subtract exponents** when dividing expressions with the same base:

$$\frac{x^5}{x^2} = \frac{x \cdot x \cdot x \cdot x \cdot x}{x \cdot x} = x^3$$

$$\frac{a^m}{a^n} = a^{m-n}$$

• **Multiply exponents** when a number raised to an exponent is raised to a second exponent:

$$(x^4)^3 = x^{4 \cdot 3} = x^{12}$$

$$(a^m)^n = a^{mn}$$

Factoring

You are likely to see questions that ask you to evaluate or compare expressions that require factoring. The types of factoring included in the math section are:

• Difference of two squares

$$a^2 - b^2 = (a + b)(a - b)$$
$$x^2 - 16 = (x + 4)(x - 4)$$
$$c^2 - 100 = (c - 10)(c + 10)$$

• Finding common factors or grouping common terms

$$8a^2x^2 + 4a^3x = 4a^2x(2x + a)$$
$$3x + 6y = 3(x + 2y)$$

• Factoring quadratics and polynomials

$$x^2 - 7x + 12 = (x - 4)(x - 3)$$
$$-2x^2 - 6x - 4 = -2(x^2 + 3x + 2)$$
$$= -2(x + 1)(x + 2)$$
$$x^2 + 2x + 1 = (x + 1)(x + 1) = (x + 1)^2$$

Solving Equations

This is one of the most important components of the exam. Algebraic expressions will appear in many different forms, ranging from simple linear equations to complex word problems. Some questions may ask you to solve for a specific value of x, while others may ask you to solve for x in terms of (an)other variable(s).

To prepare you for the exam, we will first review solving basic linear equations, systems of linear equations and inequalities, and equations involving radical expressions.

• Solving for One Variable in Terms of Another Variable

These types of questions are meant to test your understanding and use of the basic rules of arithmetic for algebraic expressions.

Example 1: If $2x + 3y = z$, what is x in terms of y and z?
   This question is asking you to isolate x by itself on one side of the equation.

   First subtract 3y from both sides.
$$2x = z - 3y$$

   Then divide both sides by 2 to get the value of x in terms of y and z.
$$x = \frac{z - 3y}{2}$$

Example 2: If $2r = 5s$ and $5s = 6t$, what does r equal in terms of t?

   Since you want to find r in terms of t, in the first equation find the value of r.
$$r = \tfrac{5}{2}s$$

   Then find s in terms of t.
$$s = \tfrac{6}{5}t$$

   Substitute the found value of s into the equation for r.
$$r = \tfrac{5}{2}(\tfrac{6}{5}t)$$

   Thus, $r = 3t$.

• Solving Quadratic Equations by Factoring

Don't be surprised if you are asked to solve quadratic equations that can be factored. You **will not** be asked to use the quadratic formula to solve these equations.

Example 1: If $x^2 + 12 = 7x$, what are the two possible values of x?

First, subtract 7x from both sides to get the standard quadratic equation.

$$x^2 - 7x + 12 = 0$$
$$(x - 4)(x - 3) = 0$$

Therefore, either $(x - 4) = 0$ or $(x - 3) = 0$. The values $x = 4$ and $x = 3$ satisfy the original equation.

Example 2: How many different solutions are there for the equation $2x + 6 = (x + 5)(x + 3)$?

    A) 0
    B) 1
    C) 2
    D) 3

First multiply the binomials.

$$2x + 6 = x^2 + 8x + 15$$

Then reorganize the terms in order to get the standard quadratic equation.

$$x^2 + 6x + 9 = 0$$
$$(x + 3)(x + 3) = 0$$

Solving for x gives a single solution of -3. Therefore the answer to the question is B, since there is only one solution, -3.

Example 3: If $\dfrac{x^2 + 7x + 12}{x + 4} = 5$, 2nd $x \neq -4$, then $x = ?$

    A) 1
    B) 2
    C) 3
    D) 5
    E) 6

First, factor the quadratic expression.

$$\frac{x^2 + 7x + 12}{x + 4} = 5$$

$$\frac{(x + 4)(x + 3)}{x + 4} = 5$$

Now we can cancel the (x + 4) terms to give x + 3 = 5. Thus, x = 2, and the answer is B.

- **Solving Algebraic Inequalities**

Definitions

An **inequality** is a statement that one quantity is greater than or less than another. Inequalities are shown using four symbols:

- Greater than: >
    $$4 > 1$$
    $$1 > -3$$
    $$2 > \sqrt{2}$$

- Greater than or equal to: ≥
    $$8/3 \geq 2$$
    $$2 + 3 \geq 5$$

- Less than: <
    $$0 < 4$$
    $$-6 < -5$$

- Less than or equal to: ≤
    $$6 - 2 \leq 5$$
    $$5/2 \leq 2.5$$

Solving inequalities works just like solving an equality, except for one important difference: **When multiplying or dividing an inequality by a negative number, you must switch.**

Example 1: Solve the inequality $2x - 5 > 9$.

> First, add 5 to both sides to give $2x > 14$. Then solve for x. The solution is $x > 7$. This expression means that all values of x greater than 7 are solutions to this inequality.

Example 2: Solve the inequality $3x + 5 < 5x - 9$.

> First, subtract 5 from both sides to give $3x < 5x - 14$. Then subtract 5x from both sides to give $-2x < -14$. To solve for x, divide both sides by -2 and switch the inequality sign to give $x > 7$ as the solution.

You may also be given graphical representations of inequalities.

Example 3: Which of the following algebraic inequalities is represented by the graph below?

A. $-2 \geq y < 2$
B. $-2 < y > 2$
C. $-2 \leq y < 2$
D. $-2 < y \leq 2$

The graph represents a line whose solution y lies between -2 and 2. The filled point represents a true value for y. Based on the graph, $y = -2$, and the open point represents $y \neq 2$. To answer the question, you must combine the two inequalities into one statement: $-2 \leq y < 2$. Therefore, the answer is C.

- **Solving Systems of Linear Equations**

You will be asked to solve systems of two or more linear equations or inequalities. Linear systems are equations that contain the same variables. Thus, $a + 2b = 11$ and $2a + b = 10$ are linear systems since they both contain the same variables, a and b.

To solve systems of linear equations, you should use the **substitution method**:
- Take one of the equations listed and find the value of one of the variables in terms of the other.
- Substitute the value found for the variable to in the other equation.
- Solve for the second variable.
- Substitute that value in to the original equation to solve for the first variable.

Example: For what values of x and y are the following equations true?

$$2x + 4y = 50$$
$$3x + 5y = 66$$

In the first equation, solve for x in terms of y.

$$2x + 4y = 50$$
$$2x = 50 - 4y$$
$$x = 25 - 2y$$

Then substitute for x in the other equation and solve for y.

$$3x + 5y = 66$$
$$3(25 - 2y) + 5y = 66$$
$$75 - 6y + 5y = 66$$
$$75 - y = 66$$
$$-y = -9$$
$$y = 9$$

Substitute y = 9 back into the original equation, 2x + 4y = 50, in order to find the value of x.

$$2x + 4(9) = 50$$
$$2x + 36 = 50$$
$$2x = 14$$
$$x = 7$$

• **Solving Radical Expressions**

The expression $2\sqrt{x}$ is a radical expression because it involves a root $^1/_M$ in this case, the square root of x.

The equation $2\sqrt{x} + 7 = 19$ is radical because it involves a radical expression.

You can solve this equation in the same way you solved other linear equations:

$$2\sqrt{x} + 7 = 19$$
$$2\sqrt{x} = 12$$
$$\sqrt{x} = 6$$
$$x = 36$$

• **Solving Absolute Value Equations and Inequalities**

Familiarity with both the concept and notation of absolute value will be helpful in solving math questions. The absolute value of a number is its distance from zero on the number line. The absolute value of the number x is denoted [x]. For example, [10] = 10 and [– 5] = 5. The absolute value of a number is never negative since it represents the value of the number regardless of charge.

You will be expected to work with expressions and solve equations that involve absolute value.

Example 1: Solve [2x – 3] > 5.

The first thing to do is clear the absolute value bars by splitting the inequality into two:

$$[2x - 3] > 5$$
$$2x - 3 < -5 \text{ or } 2x - 3 > 5$$

Then solve for x in each equation.

$$2x < -2 \text{ or } 2x > 8$$
$$x < -1 \text{ or } x > 4$$

Thus, the solution to $[2x - 3] > 5$ consists of the $x < -1$ or $x > 4$.

On a graph, this would be represented as the number line shown, below with open points at -1 and 4, and arrows pointing in opposite directions to show $x < -1$ and $x > 4$.

• **Solving Rational Expressions**

A **rational expression** is the quotient of two polynomials (written as a fraction). For example:

$$\frac{x - 1}{x - 2}$$

You will likely be asked to solve equations or inequalities involving such expressions.

Example: For what value of x is the following equation true?

$$\frac{4x}{2x - 1} = 5$$

First multiply both sides by $2x - 1$ to put the equation in linear form.

$$\frac{4x}{2x - 1}(2x - 1) = 5(2x - 1)$$

$$4x = 10x - 5$$

Solve for x.

$$-6x = -5$$
$$x = {}^5/_6$$

Functions

A function is a rule or formula that tells how to relate elements in one set (the domain) with the elements in another set (the range). There are many different types of function notations that you should be familiar with. Here are a few examples:

$$y = x^2$$
$$f(x) = \sqrt{x} - 3$$
$$g(x) = 2^x + 1/x$$

In each case, a specific value of x will give you a specific value of y, f(x), or g(x).

Example 1: Given $f(x) = x^2 + 2x - 1$, find $f(2)$.

When you see a question like this, all you need to do is substitute the new x value into the function. In this case, substitute 2 for x in the function.

$$f(2) = (2)^2 + 2(2) - 1$$
$$= 4 + 4 - 1$$
$$= 7$$

Example 2: Given $f(x) = \begin{cases} 2x^2 - 1 \text{ for } x < 1 \\ x + 4 \text{ for } x \geq 1 \end{cases}$, find $f(0)$ and $f(1)$.

This is called a "piecewise" function. The function is split into two halves: the half that comes before $x = 1$ and the half that goes from $x = 1$ to infinity. Which half of the function that you use depends on the value of x. If we evaluate $f(0)$, we must use the first function, since $0 < 1$. Then $f(0) = 2(0)^2 - 1 = 0$. If we evaluate $f(1)$, we must use the second half of the function, since $x \geq 1$. Therefore, $f(1) = (1) + 4 = 5$.

Example 3: Given that $f(x) = 3x^2 + 2x$, find $f(x + h)$.

Everywhere there is an x, plug in x + h.

$$f(x) = 3x^2 + 2x$$
$$f(x + h) = 3(x + h^2) + 2x + h$$
$$= 3(x^2 + 2xh + h^2) + 2x + 2h$$
$$= 3x^2 + 6xh + 3h^2 + 2x + 2h$$

Domain and Range

- The **domain** of a function is the set of all the values for which the function is defined.
- The **range** of a function is the set of all the values that are the output, or result, of applying the function.

Example: What are the domain and range of $f(x) = -\sqrt{-2x+3}$?

In this example, the domain is all the values that x can be. The only rule of this function is that you cannot take the root of a negative number. Therefore, by definition, $-2x + 3 \geq 0$.

First, to find all acceptable values of x, solve for x in $-2x + 3 \geq 0$.

$$-2x + 3 \geq 0$$
$$-2x \geq -3$$
$$x \leq 3/2$$

Thus, the domain is "all $x \leq 3/2$."

To find the range in this example, plug in the highest value for x, which is $3/2$. Thus, $f^{3}/_{2} = 0$. For any other value of x, f(x) will be negative. Therefore, the range is $f(x) \leq 0$.

Practice Problems for Manipulating Algebraic Expressions

1) If $x = -3$, then $4x^2 - 3x - 7 = ?$

   A) −34
   B) 20
   C) 34
   D) 38
   E) 52

2) If $3x + 5y = 6$ and $2x + y = 4$, then what is x?

   A) 2
   B) 0
   C) −1
   D) 4
   E) 5

3) Evaluate $\sqrt{25a^2}$.

   A) 5
   B) 2a
   C) 25
   D) 5a
   E) $5a^2$

4) Factor 6x² – 12x + 6 completely.

    A) 6(x – 1)(x + 2)
    B) – 6(-x + 4)(x + 2)
    C) 6(x – 1)(x – 1)
    D) 3(2x – 1)(x – 2)
    E) 2(3x + 2)(x + 1)

5) What is a possible solution of [2x – 3] – 4 = 3?

    A) 2
    B) – 2
    C) – 5
    D) 1
    E) 3

6) Solve the following equation:

$$\frac{x-1}{15} = \frac{2}{5}$$

    A) 3
    B) 4
    C) 5
    D) 6
    E) 7

Note: Answers may be found on page 108.

How Things Change: Ratios, Proportions, and Variations

This section deals with ratios, proportions, and how a quantity changes with regard to another quantity (variation). The topics build upon each other. Proportions are merely statements of equality involving ratios, and variation problems will often be written as proportions. Whether you are aware of it or not, you use ratios every day. When you talk about the rate of travel of a vehicle being 45 mph, you are talking about the ratio of distance traveled to time traveled.

Ratios and Proportions

Ratios are used to compare two quantities. They are typically written in one of two ways: as a fraction or with a colon (:). The ratio read as "4 to 10" could be written as 4/10 or as 4:10. The ratio expressing the relationship between a day and a week would be written as 1/7 or 1:7 because there are seven days in a week.

A proportion is a mathematical statement equating two ratios. Two ratios are said to be equal if, when written in fractional form, the fractions are equivalent fractions. We will compare and solve ratios using *cross multiplication*. If the cross products are equal, the ratios are equal. Take a look at the example below.

$$\frac{x-1}{2} = \frac{x+2}{3}$$

Cross multiply and solve for x.

$$3(x - 1) = 2(x + 2)$$
$$3x - 3 = 2x + 4$$
$$-2x \qquad -2x$$
$$x - 3 = 4$$
$$-3 \quad +3$$
$$x = 7$$

The correct answer is x = 7. We can check our answer by plugging it back into the original proportion.

$$\frac{7-1}{2} = \frac{7+2}{3}$$

$$\frac{6}{2} = \frac{9}{3}$$

$$3 = 3$$

The final statement, 3 = 3, is a true statement. Therefore, x = 7 is the correct answer. If you noticed that 6/2 and 9/3 are equivalent fractions, you could have stopped at this point. Two ratios are equal if their fractional forms are equivalent fractions. Remember, you may have to rewrite the proportion in fractional form before you solve it.

Solve for x : x: 6 = 4 : 12

Begin by rewriting the problem in fractional form and then solve for x as we did above.

$$\frac{x}{6} = \frac{4}{12}$$
$$12x = 6 \bullet 4$$
$$12x = 24$$
$$/12 \quad /12$$
$$x = 2$$

You probably could have solved this problem by observation. Recognizing that 4/12 is simply 1/3, we know that the left-hand side must be equal to 1/3 as well. One-third of 5 is 2. You may find that simple observations such as this will provide significant time savings on the exam.

Variations

Variations deal with explaining, in mathematical language, how one quantity changes with respect to one or more other quantities. The amount of flour needed in a bread recipe varies with the number of loaves being made. The time it takes to paint a house varies with the number of people doing the work. The first is an example of *direct variation*; the second, of *inverse variation*.

In the example of direct variation given above, the amount of flour needed for the recipe will vary directly with the number of loaves being made. Making more loaves will require more flour; making fewer loaves will require less flour. In direct variation the variables will move in the same direction. As one variable increases or decreases, the other variable will move in the same direction. These problems can be solved using proportions. Consider the example problem below.

> If it takes 3 gallons of paint to cover 100 ft²,
> how many gallons of paint will be needed to cover 600 ft²?

The problem gives us the ratio of 3 gallons of paint to every 100 ft². We can use this to set up a proportion problem.

$$\frac{3}{100} = \frac{x}{600}$$

$$100x = 3 \cdot 600$$

$$100x = 1800$$

$$\frac{100x}{100} = \frac{1800}{100}$$

$$x = 18$$

It will take 18 gallons of paint to cover 600 ft². When we say "y varies directly as x," we could also write:

$$y = kx$$

where k is called the *constant of variation*. In the previous problem, the number of gallons of paint varies directly with the square footage that will be covered. The constant of variation is 3/100. We would then have

$$y = \frac{3}{100} x$$

$$= \frac{3}{100} \cdot 600$$

$$= 18$$

When two variables or quantities change in opposite directions, this is an example of *inverse variation*. In the example above about painting a house, the time required to paint the house *varies inversely with* the number of people painting. This means that the more people painting the house, the less total time it will take to paint. When we say "y varies inversely with x," we can express this as:

$$y = \frac{k}{x}$$

Again, **k is the constant of variation**. We can find, k by simply multiplying the known values for the two variables. Consider the example below.

> A particular hotel has a custodial staff of 12 employees, and they can typically clean all of the hotel rooms in 6 hours. If four members of the custodial staff are not at work today, how long will it take the remaining custodians to clean all of the hotel rooms?

In the example above, the total time taken to complete the job is inversely proportional to the number of workers. The constant of variation, k, is simply $6 \cdot 12 = 72$. We can thus solve the problem as below.

$$y = \frac{72}{x}$$
$$= \frac{72}{8}$$
$$= 9$$

The correct answer is 9 hours. I hope you recognized that the number of workers present is 8. There are 4 custodians absent, so $x = 12 - 4 = 8$. Be sure to read the information provided in the problems carefully.

Two additional types of variation problems that we will discuss are *joint variation* and *combined variation*. These are just extensions of direct and inverse variation. When we say that "y varies jointly with x and z," we have an example of *joint variation*. This can be written as:

$$y = kxz,$$

where k is again the constant of variation. The constant of variation is simply the ratio of y to x and z (x times z). Consider the problem below.

> The variable y varies jointly with x and z.
> The value of y is 12 when x is 4 and z is 8.
> What is y when $x = 6$ and $z = 10$?

First, we want to be sure that we recognize the type of variation that is present. It is pretty simple for this problem: "y varies jointly with x and z." We thus have the form:

$$y = kxy,$$

and we simply need to determine the value for the constant of variation, k.

$$k = \frac{y}{xy}$$

$$= \frac{12}{4 \cdot 8}$$

$$= \frac{3}{8}$$

Now, we simply plug this into the equation of variation and solve for our unknown.

$$k = \frac{3}{8} xy$$

$$= \frac{3}{8} \cdot 6 \cdot 10$$

$$= \frac{45}{2}$$

$$= 22 \, {}^{1}/_{2}$$

The correct answer is $22 \, {}^{1}/_{2}$.

Combined variation involves both direct and inverse variation. For example, if we say "y varies directly with x and inversely with z," this is an example of combined variation. This can be written, similar to the joint variations previously presented, as

$$y = k \frac{x}{z}$$

Consider the following example:

It takes 2 hours for 3 people to paint 100 ft. of 6-ft. fencing.
Assuming that each person is capable of painting at the same rate,
how long will it take for 12 people to paint 1,800 ft. of the same fencing?

The total time (t) needed to paint a section of fencing is directly proportional to the length of the fence (l) and inversely proportional to the number of people (n) who are painting.

$$t = k\frac{l}{n}$$

We simply need to determine the constant of variation, k.

$$k = \frac{tn}{l}$$

$$= \frac{2 \cdot 3}{100}$$

$$= \frac{6}{100}$$

Now that we have k, we need to insert it into the equation of variation to get the answer.

$$t = \frac{6}{100} \times \frac{l}{n}$$

$$= \frac{6}{100} \times \frac{1800}{12}$$

$$= 9$$

The correct answer is 9 hours.

Ratios, Proportions, and Variation Practice Problems

1) Which of the following ratios represent the relationship of hours to days?

   I. 24/1   IV. 1/24
   II. 1:24   V. 24:1
   III. 1 to 24

   A) I, III, and V   D) I and V
   B) II, III, and IV   E) II and IV
   C) II, III, and V

2) There are 14 boys and 16 girls in Tyler's class. Which ratio best represents the relationship between the number of boys and the number of students in Tyler's class?

   A) 7/8   D) 14:16
   B) 7:10   E) 8:15
   C) 7/15

3) The ratio of $f(x)$ to $g(x)$ is $3:x+2$. If $f(x) = x - 2$, what is $g(x)$ in terms of x?

   A) $3x - 6$ D) $3x^2 - 12$
   B) $\frac{1}{3}(x^2 - 2)$ E) $\frac{1}{3}(x^2 - 4)$
   C) $\frac{2}{3}x$

4) If the ratio of A to B is 3:4 and the ratio of B to C is 2:3, what is the value of A when C is 5?

   A) 10   D) 5
   B) 3/2   E) 6
   C) 5/2

5) If y varies directly with x and y = 4, what is the value of y when x = 7/11?

   A) 4/11   D) 44/49
   B) $2\frac{3}{4}$ E) $1\frac{5}{49}$
   C) 11/18

6) If x varies inversely with y and y = 8 when x = 3, what is the value of x when y = 12?

   A) 9/4   D) 2
   B) 1/2   E) 4/9
   C) $4\frac{1}{2}$

7) The variable s varies jointly with t and u such that s = 7 when t = 4 and u = 3. What is the constant of variation describing the relationship between s on the one hand and t and u on the other?

    A) 84   D) 21/4

    B) 12/7   E) 7/12

    C) 4/21

8) The value of w varies directly with x and y and inversely with z. The constant of variation is 13/7. What is the value of z when w = 13 and y = 3?

    A) 6/7   D) 7/6

    B) 7/13   E) 13/7

    C) 6/13

Note: Answers may be found on Page 113.

Playing the odds: Probability and Statistics

Some questions you are sure to encounter on the *SAT* math section will invoke your ability to calculate the likelihood (probability) of an event occurring and your ability to work with basic statistical measures (mean, median, and mode). We'll review here a few of the most important concepts that you will need to be successful on these questions.

Probability

When answering these problems, keep in mind that the probability can be any number from 0 to 1 inclusive. If an event is not possible (cannot ever occur), the probability is 0. If an event is certain (will always occur), the probability is 1. You will never have a probability that is less than 0 or greater than 1. The probability formula can be used to calculate the probability of an event occurring.

$$\text{Probability} = \frac{\text{Number of times an event can occur}}{\text{Total number of possible outcomes}}$$

The probability is simply the ratio of the number of successful events divided by the total number of possible events. In a deck of 52 playing cards, the probability of pulling one of the sixteen face cards is 16/52 or 4/13. In contrast, the probability of drawing one of the four jacks is 4/52 or 1/13.

Dependent and Independent Events

Calculating the probability of a single event is typically pretty simple. However, you may be asked to calculate the probability that two (or possibly more) events will both occur. In order to answer such a question, you will need to understand the difference between *dependent* and *independent* events. Events are considered *dependent* if the outcome of one event affects the probability of the other event. To calculate the probability of dependent events, we have to use something known as the *conditional probability*. The conditional probability is the probability that an event will occur given that one or more other events have occurred. Take the generic example of three dependent events (A, B, and C). The probability that all three events will occur is given by the following expression

$$P(A,B,C) = P(A) \bullet P(B\backslash A) \bullet P(C\backslash A,B).$$

Don't let this expression scare you. $P(A)$ is simply the probability that event A will occur. $P(B\backslash A)$ is the probability that event B will occur given that event A has occurred. Likewise, $P(C\backslash A,B)$ is the probability that event C will occur if events A and B have occurred. The probability that all three events will occur, $P(A,B,C)$, is simply the product of these three terms. This can be generalized to include more than three events. This will make more sense to you with an example.

> This weekend is the first round of the regional middle school soccer tournament. On Saturday morning, the team from Madris will play against the team from Dekalb. In the afternoon, Madris will play against the team from Fulton. On Sunday afternoon, Dekalb will play against Fulton. In each game, either team has a 50 percent chance of winning the game. What is the probability that Madris will win both of its games and Fulton will lose both of its games?

To solve this problem, we will have to use conditional probabilities. The probability that Madris will win its first game is $1/2$. The probability that Madris will win its second game (against Fulton) is *independent* of the outcome of its first game. So, the conditional probability that Madris wins its second game given that it won its first game is still $1/2$. The probability that Fulton will lose its first game is $1/2$, but the conditional probability that Fulton will lose its first game given that Madris won both of its games is actually 1. Madris plays against Fulton in this game, so if we are given that Madris won this game then we know that Fulton lost this game. The probability that Fulton loses its second game is $1/2$. Notice that this is also conditional probability. The likelihood that Fulton will lose its second game is independent of whether Madris won its games and independent of whether Fulton lost its first game. The probability that all four events occur (Madris wins its games and Fulton loses its games) is just the product of these probabilities.

$$P(A,B,C,D) = P(A) \bullet P(B/A) \bullet P(C/A,B) \bullet P(D/A,B,C)$$

$$= \frac{1}{2} \bullet \frac{1}{2} \bullet 1 \bullet \frac{1}{2} = \frac{1}{8}$$

The correct answer is 1/8. This also clarifies another concept, that of *independent events*. Take the first two events in the above problem for example. Madris, winning its first game and Madris, winning its second game are independent events. Events are considered independent if the outcome of one event has no effect on the likelihood of the other. The probability of two independent events is simply the product of the respective probabilities for these events. The probability that Madris will win both of its games is $\frac{1}{2} \cdot \frac{1}{2}$, or $\frac{1}{4}$.

Statistics

There won't be too many problems that cover statistics on the test, but you can be sure there will be at least one. It is highly unlikely that any will cover topics beyond the three most basic statistical measures: mean (arithmetic average), median, and mode. The mean of a set of n numbers is just the sum of the numbers divided by n (the number of items in the set). To find the average of 15, 21, and 39 you would do the following:

$$\frac{15 + 21 + 39}{3} = \frac{75}{3} = 25$$

You may have to rely on your understanding of the properties of averages to arrive at an answer on the test when directly calculating the averages is difficult or time consuming. The average of two numbers is halfway between the two numbers on a number line. The average of 3 and 5 is 4. When you have a set of numbers evenly spaced, the average will simply be the middle number. The average of the first nine odd numbers will simply be the 5th odd number, or 9. When there is an even number of terms in the set, the average is just the average of the two middle numbers. The average of the first 100 odd numbers is just the average of the 50th (99) and 51st (101) odd numbers. So the average is 100.

Two concepts that often appear on the test deal with weighted averages and finding a missing number when an average is given. The average of a set of numbers is just the sum of the numbers divided by the number of terms in the set.

$$\text{Average} = \frac{\text{Sum of terms}}{\text{\# of terms}}$$

Likewise, we can use the average and the number of terms to calculate the sum of the terms.

Sum of terms = (Average) x (# of terms)

This principle is central to both calculating a missing term and to the concept of a weighted average. If we are given the value for three of the four terms (17, 35, 39) and the average (34), we can calculate the value of the missing term.

Sum of terms = 17 + 35 + 39 + x = 34 x 4 = 136

91 + x = 136

x = 45

If we are given that (in a class of 16 girls and 13 boys) the boys averaged 75 on the last exam and the girls averaged 83, we can calculate the class average using a weighted average. Note that the average is not just the average of the boys' and girls' test averages.

$$\text{Class Average} = \frac{\text{Sum of Boy's Scores} + \text{Sum of Girl's Scores}}{\text{total \# of students}}$$

$$= \frac{(\text{Boys, Average}) \times (\text{\# of Boys}) + (\text{Girls, Average}) \times (\text{\# of Girls})}{\text{\# of Boys} + \text{\# of Girls}}$$

$$= \frac{75 \times 13 + 83 \times 16}{13 + 16} = \frac{975 + 1328}{29} = \frac{2303}{29} = 79.4$$

The average is slightly closer to 83 than it is to 75 because there are more girls in the class than boys.

Probability and Statistics Practice Problems

1) If a pair of fair dice is tossed, what is the probability that the sum of the two numbers is 4?

    A) 1/6   D) 1/18
    B) 1/12   E) 1/9
    C) 1/2

2) If a pair of fair dice is tossed, what is the probability that the sum of the two numbers is an even number less than 10?

    A) 1/3   D) 7/18
    B) 1/2   E) 2/3
    C) 4/11

Note: Answers may be found on page 108.

Measuring Up: Geometry

This section deals with the relationships between points, lines, and angles and the figures they form. The *SAT* has many questions involving the topics in this section. After algebra, this is the next most important section on the exam. Understanding the concepts will enable you to answer 30-40% of the questions that you will see on the exam.

Definitions of Lines and Angles

A line extends forever in either direction. The line below, called l, has three collinear points on it: A, B, and C. The part of the line between points A and B is called a line segment. In this instance, the line segment between points A and B will be referred to as either "segment AB" or simply $\overline{AB}$. A and B are the endpoints of segment AB.

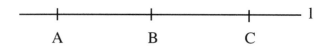

Angles are most often described by the points on the lines that intersect to form the angle or by the point of intersection itself. For instance, in the diagram below, angle ABC could be described as either $\angle ABC$ or $\angle x$.

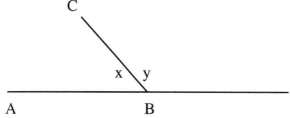

A line forms an angle of 180°. If that line is cut by another line, it divides the 180° into two pieces that together add up to 180° ($\angle x + \angle y = 180°$). Two angles that when added together make 180° are called supplementary angles ($\angle x$ and $\angle y$ are **supplementary** to each other).

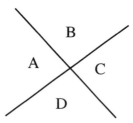

When two lines intersect, they form four angles, represented above by the letters A, B, C, and D. $\angle A$ and $\angle B$ together form a straight line, so they add up to 180°. The same is true for $\angle C$ and $\angle D$, $\angle A$ and $\angle D$, or $\angle B$ and $\angle C$. Since there are 180° above the line ($\angle A + \angle B$), there are also 180° below the line (($\angle C + \angle D$). Therefore, the sum of the four angles is 360°. $\angle A$ and $\angle C$ are opposite from each other and always equal to each other, as are $\angle B$ and $\angle D$. These are known as **vertical angles**. In the figure below, $\angle x = \angle y = 60°$.

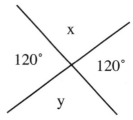

When two lines meet so that 90° angles are formed, the lines are said to be **perpendicular** to each other. The 90° angle is called a **right angle**. A right angle is represented by a little box at the point of intersection of the two lines. The perpendicularity of lines l_2 and l_2 in the figure below is represented as $l_1 \perp l_2$.

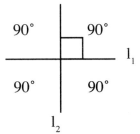

Two angles whose sum is 90°, or one right angle, are said to be **complementary**. For instance, in the figure below, ∠AOB is the complement of ∠BOC. Thus, ∠AOB + ∠BOC = 90°.

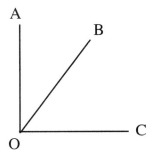

Two lines in the same plane that are equally distant from one another at all points are called parallel lines. Parallel lines never meet. Parallel lines are often represented as $l_1 \parallel l_2$.

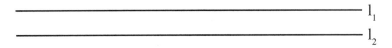

When parallel lines are cut by a third line (known as a transversal), eight angles are formed.

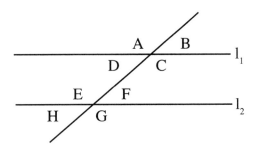

Based on what you've learned about parallel lines, $\angle A = \angle C$ and $\angle B = \angle D$. Since the same transversal cuts line l_2, the four angles $\angle E$, $\angle F$, $\angle G$, and $\angle H$ are in the same proportions as the angles above. Thus, $\angle E = \angle A$ and $\angle F = \angle B$. The next figure shows an example of the relationship of parallel lines cut by a transversal.

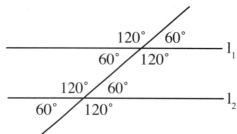

Triangles

A triangle is a three-sided figure whose angles always add up to 180°. The largest angle of a triangle is opposite its longest side. On the exam, the triangle below will be represented as either triangle abc or $\triangle abc$.

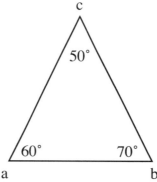

On the exam, you will be expected to recognize specific types of triangles and understand the particular properties of each kind. Each kind is listed below with an explanation of the properties that you are expected to know.

• **Equilateral Triangles**

The three sides of an equilateral triangle are equal in length (a = b = c). The three angles are also equal; therefore, since the three angles of a triangle must add up to 180°, each angle of an equilateral triangle must equal 60° (x = y = z = 60°).

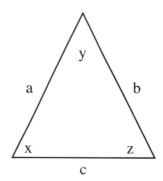

• **Isosceles Triangles**

An isosceles triangle is a triangle with two sides of equal length (a = b). The angles opposite the equal sides are also equal (x = y).

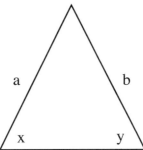

• **Right Triangles**

A right triangle is a triangle with a right angle. Therefore, the other angles are by definition, complementary angles (∠Y + ∠Z = 90°). The longest side of a right triangle (the one opposite the 90° angle) is called the **hypotenuse** (yz or side c in the figure below). The other sides are often referred to as **legs**.

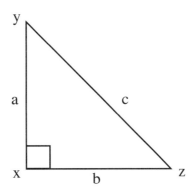

Of all the triangles on the exam, right triangles appear the most often. Much information can be obtained from figures that contain right triangles due to the fact that their sides always exist in a particular proportion to each other. This proportion is better known as the **Pythagorean theorem**. (Note: Understanding this theorem is central to being successful on the exam.)

  * The Pythagorean theorem is expressed in the following equation:

$$a^2 + b^2 = c^2,$$

where c^2 is always the square of the hypotenuse (the side opposite the right angle) and $a^2 + b^2$ is the sum of the squares of the other sides.

If you know the lengths of any two sides of a right triangle, you can use this equation to find the length of the last side.

Remember: 1) the hypotenuse will always be the longest side, and 2) this works only for right triangles. In other words, if the triangle does not have a right angle, you **cannot** use the Pythagorean Theorem.

There are several "special" right triangles that frequently appear on the exam:

30°-60°-90° Triangles

The lengths of a 30°-60°-90° triangle are in the ratio of $1:\sqrt{3}:2$, as shown in the figure below.

Short leg = x
Long leg = $x\sqrt{3}$
Hypotenuse = 2x

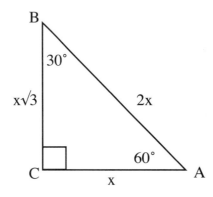

For example, if you know the length of the hypotenuse is 4 and the length of the short leg is 2, then the Pythagorean theorem gives you the length of the longer leg:

$$c^2 = a^2 + b^2$$
$$c = 4, a = 2$$
$$4^2 = 2^2 + b^2$$
$$16 = 4 + b^2$$
$$12 = b^2$$
$$b = 2\sqrt{3}$$

45°-45°-90° Triangles

A 45°-45°-90° triangle is an isosceles triangle containing a right angle. Thus, the two legs of the triangle (opposite the 45° angles) are equal. The sides of the triangle are in the ratio of $1:1:\sqrt{2}$, as shown in the figure below.

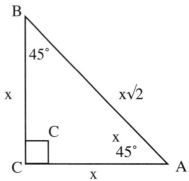

• **Area of a Triangle**

The **area of a triangle** is defined as half the base (b) of the triangle times the height (h) of the triangle, which is represented by the formula below:

$$\text{area}\,\Delta = \tfrac{1}{2}bh$$

Height is the perpendicular distance from the base of the triangle to its highest point.

In the first two triangles below, the height is represented by a dashed line. The height of the triangle can be outside the triangle itself, as in the second example below. In the right triangle, the base and height are just the legs of the triangle.

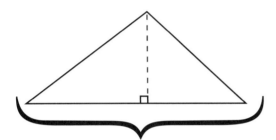 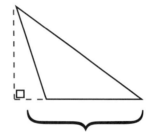 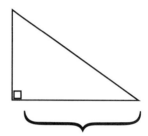

• **Similar and Congruent Triangles**

Two triangles are **similar** if their angles have the same measure. The triangles therefore have the same shape, and their sides will be in proportion. For example, the two triangles below are similar. Both are 45°- 45°- 90° right triangles; therefore, each side of one triangle is in proportion to the corresponding side of the other triangle. Here, the first triangle is three times as large as the second triangle, since the sides are in a ratio of 3:1.

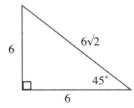

Two triangles are similar if:
1) Two pairs of corresponding angles have the same measure.
2) One pair of corresponding angles has the same measure, and the pairs of corresponding sides that form those angles have lengths that are in the same ratio.

Congruent triangles are triangles that have the same size and shape.

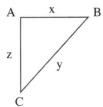 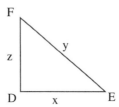

Each side of △ABC has the same length as the corresponding side of △DEF.

$$AB = DE = x$$
$$BC = EF = y$$
$$CA = FD = z$$

Each angle of △ABC is equal to its corresponding angle in △DEF.

Here's a quick checklist to determine if two triangles are congruent.

1) Each pair of corresponding sides has the same length.
2) Two pairs of corresponding sides each have the same length, and the angles formed by these sides have the same measure.
3) One pair of corresponding sides has the same length, and two pairs of corresponding angles each have the same measure.

Note: If any of these three details is true, then you're dealing with two congruent triangles.

Quadrilaterals and Other Polygons

A **quadrilateral** is a four-sided polygon whose angle measures sum to equal 360°. There are several types of quadrilaterals that you will see on the exam. You will be expected to utilize the information that these figures offer in order to solve many types of questions.

The **perimeter** of any polygon is the sum of the lengths of its sides.

The most common four-sided figures are the rectangle and the square, followed by the parallelogram and the trapezoid.

• **Parallelograms**

A parallelogram is a four-sided figure in which both pairs of opposite sides are parallel, both pairs of opposite angles are equal, and both pairs of opposite sides are equal in length.

The area of a parallelogram is its base times its height, but due to its shape, the height of a parallelogram is not always equal to one of its sides. To find the height of a parallelogram, you must draw a perpendicular line from the base to the top of the figure.

Area of a parallelogram = base x height

• **Rectangles and Squares**

A rectangle is a parallelogram that has four interior angles that are each equal to 90°. Opposite sides of a rectangle are equal. The diagonal of a rectangle makes two equal right triangles. The Pythagorean theorem can be used to figure out details regarding the length of sides or the diagonal depending on what information you're given. The area of a rectangle is its length times its width. In the figure below, the area = 6 x 3, or 18.

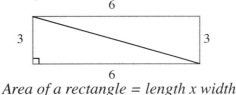

Area of a rectangle = length x width

A square is a type of rectangle whose four sides are equal in length. It is important to notice that the diagonal of a square makes two 45°-45°-90° triangles with the sides of the square. Thus, you can figure out the length of the sides from the length of the diagonal or the length of the diagonal from the length of a side.

Since a square is a rectangle, the area of a square is also length times width. However, since each side s is the same, the area of a square can be represented as:

Area of a square = s^2

• **Trapezoids**

A trapezoid is a quadrilateral having one pair of parallel sides.
Since $\overline{AB}$ // $\overline{DC}$, x + y = 180° and w + z = 180°.

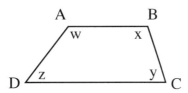

The easiest way to find the area of a trapezoid is to divide it into two triangles and a rectangle, figure out the areas of the individual pieces, and then add the results together to find the area of the whole figure.

Circles

A circle represents all the points at a distance of r away from any given point. The measure of degrees around the point of

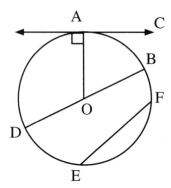

- **Definitions**

A **chord** is a line connecting two points on a circle ($\overline{BD}$ and $\overline{EF}$ are chords). The **diameter** of a circle is a line segment that passes through the center and has its endpoints on the circle, as in $\overline{DOB}$. All diameters of the same circle have equal length.

The **radius** of a circle is a line segment extending from the center of the circle to a point on the circle. All radii of the same circle have equal length ($\overline{OA}$ and $\overline{OB}$ are both radii). The radius is also half the diameter.

An **arc** is a part of a circle. An arc can be measured in degrees or in units of length. (AB is an arc.) If you form an angle by drawing radii from the ends of the arc to the center of the circle, the number of degrees in the arc equals the number of degrees in the angle formed.

A **tangent** to a circle is a line that touches the circle at only one point. A tangent is always perpendicular to the radius that contains the point of the line that touches the circle. $\overline{AC}$ is a tangent to circle O.

The **circumference** is the measure of the distance around the circle. It is equal to π times the diameter, d (or π times twice the radius, r).

$$Circumference = \pi d$$
$$or$$
$$Circumference = 2\pi r$$

The area of a circle is equal to π times the square of the radius.

$$Area\ of\ a\ circle = \pi r^2$$

Graphing and Coordinate Geometry

You will be expected to answer questions involving both linear and quadratic equations and their graphs. Therefore, you will need to understand the basics of the coordinate plane.

• **The Cartesian Grid**

Every real point (x,y) has a place on this grid. For instance, the point A (3,1) can be found by counting over on the x-axis three places to the right of the origin (0,0) and then counting on the y-axis one place up from the origin.

Note: Always remember: moving up on a grid means x is becoming more positive, while moving left on a grid means y is becoming more positive. For instance, when moving from point C to point B, you must go from –2 to 2 on the x-axis and from –3 to –1 on the y-axis.

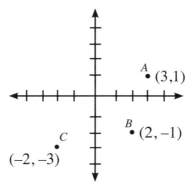

The Cartesian grid can be broken up into four quadrants with respect to the x-axis and y-axis. The signs of x and y change depending on the quadrant which the point lies. The quadrants are labeled from I to IV in a counterclockwise direction. In Quadrant I (top right), both x and y are positive. In Quadrant II (top left), y is positive whereas x is negative. In Quadrant III (bottom left), the values of both x and y are negative. Finally, in Quadrant IV (bottom right), x is positive while y is negative. The importance of this concept will become more apparent later when reflecting points or lines are discussed, since the signs in Quadrants I and III are exact opposites (the same is true for Quadrants II and IV).

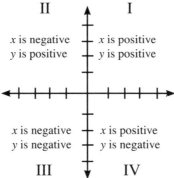

Finding the midpoint between two points

You will be expected to find the midpoint of line segments in the coordinate plane. The midpoint (xm, ym) is the average of the x's and average of the y's:

$$x_m = \frac{x_1 + x_2}{2} \qquad y_m = \frac{y_1 + y_2}{2}$$

For instance, if $\overline{AB}$ has endpoints A (4,5) and B (2,3), then the midpoint of $\overline{AB}$ has the coordinates:

$$(\frac{4+2}{2} \bullet \frac{5+3}{2}) = (3,4)$$

Finding the distance between two points

The Pythagorean Theorem can be used to find the distance between any two points in the coordinate plane. Take the figure below.

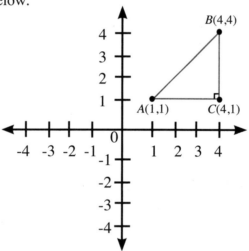

Points A, B, and C form a right triangle, $\triangle ABC$, where AC = 3 and CB = 3. (Thus, $\triangle ABC$ is an isosceles right triangle.) Applying the Pythagorean theorem:

$$AB^2 = 3^2 + 3^2$$
$$AB^2 = 18$$
$$AB = \sqrt{18} = 3\sqrt{2}$$

Therefore, the distance between two points (x_1, y_1) and (x_2, y_2) in the coordinate plane can be summarized by the formula:

$$\textit{Distance between two points} = \sqrt{(x_2 - x_1)^2 + (y_2 - y_1)^2}$$

• **Equations of lines (y-intercept form)**

The equation of a line can be found by using the following formula:

$$y = mx + b,$$

where x and y are represented by the point (x, y), m is the **slope** of the line (how sharply a line is inclining or declining), and b is the **y-intercept** (the point where a line crosses the y-axis).

The **slope of a line** between two points (x_1, y_1) and (x_2, y_2) is defined as:

$$Slope = \frac{rise}{run} = \frac{change\ in\ y}{change\ in\ x} = \frac{y_1 - y_2}{x_1 - x_2}$$

Below is the graph of the line y = 2x + 1. The line crosses the y-axis at a point 1 above the origin (y = 1). The slope is 2. An easy way to think of the slope is as the fraction $^2/_1$, where 2 represents the direction of movement on the y-axis and 1 represents the direction of movement on the x-axis. Thus, from y = 1 on the y-axis, you would move up 2 and right 1.

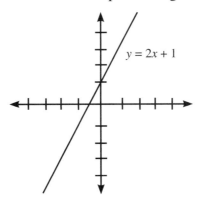

If the equation of a line is y = $-^3/_2$x − 1, you would start by moving 1 down from the origin to y = −1. If you interpret the fraction as $^{-3}/_2$, then you would move 3 down and 2 to the right to give you the graph shown below.

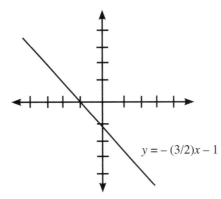

Key relationships

A **positive slope** represents an inclining line (y values increase from left to right).

A **negative slope** represents a declining line (y values decrease from left to right).

Parallel lines have **equal** slopes. For instance, the lines y = 3x + 1 and y = 3x – 2 are parallel lines because both lines have a slope of 3.

Two lines are **perpendicular** when the product of their slopes equals –1. The lines y = 2x + 1 and y = –$\frac{1}{2}$x – 3 are perpendicular lines because the product of their slopes equals –1 (1 • (–$\frac{1}{2}$) = –1).

• **Graphs of Quadratic Functions**

You will be expected to be able to identify some of the features of the graph of a quadratic equation, such as its highest or lowest point, its solutions, and its direction.

The equation of a quadratic function is expressed as

$$y = ax^2 + bx + c$$

where a, b, and c are all constants and a ≠ 0.

The graph of a quadratic function is called a **parabola**. A parabola is a U-shaped curve that can open upward or downward depending on the sign of a. If a > 0, then the graph will open upward. If a < 0, then the graph will open downward.

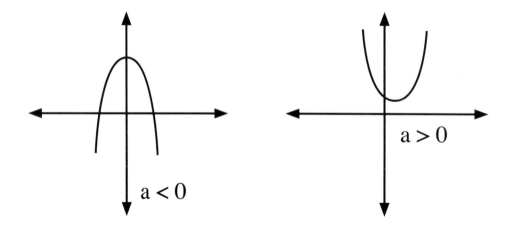

Transformations

• **Important terms**

A **translation** is described as a linear movement that does not involve any rotations or reflections. In the figure below, the line segment has been translated 2 to the units right (in the positive x-direction).

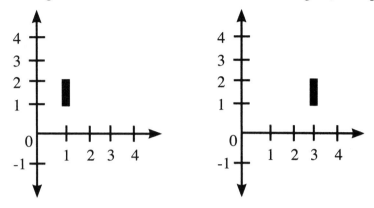

When a figure is **rotated**, it is turned around a central point, or point of rotation. The first rectangle below has been rotated 90° to create the second rectangle.

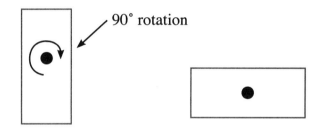

When an object is reflected, its mirror image is produced with respect to a line (called the line of reflection). The left triangle in the figure below has been reflected about line *l* to create the right triangle. The two are mirror images.

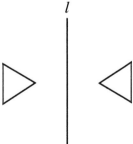

• **Symmetry**

When a figure can be folded such that each half matches the other exactly, the figure is said to possess a degree of symmetry. The line on which the figure is folded to give the equal halves is called a **line** or **axis of symmetry**. Line *l* is one axis of symmetry in the figure below.

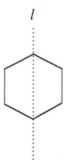

When a figure is rotated and the resulting figure is the same as the original figure, the figure is said to possess symmetry about a point (**point of symmetry**). A rotation of 180° of the figure below will yield the same figure.

Note: Symmetry about a point and symmetry about a line are different properties. A given figure may have either type of symmetry, both types of symmetry, or neither type.

Geometry Practice Problems

1) What is the perimeter of a rectangle with a 7-inch width and a 16-inch length?
    A) 32 inches
    B) 63 inches
    C) 23 inches
    D) 46 inches
    E) 54 inches

2) What is the radius of a circle with a 314-yard circumference?
    A) 10 yards
    B) 22 yards
    C) 50 yards
    D) 24 yards
    E) 100 yards

3) What is the slope of the equation 2y + 17 = 8x?

   A) 8
   B) – 4
   C) 4
   D) 14
   E) 17

4) Three vertices of a parallelogram are at (2,1), (–1,–3), and (6,4). Which of the following could be the coordinates of the remaining vertex?

   A) (0,3)
   B) (3,0)
   C) (–1,4)
   D) (6,1)
   E) (4,–1)

5) In the triangle below, YZ // MN. MX = 5, NX = 9, MY = x – 2, and NZ = x + 6. What is the length of YX?

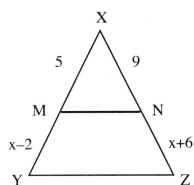

   A) 10
   B) 12
   C) 15
   D) 18
   E) 21

Note: Answers may be found on page 108.

Is This a Foreign Language?
- Mathematical Terminology and Word Problems

Some problems in the math section will be presented as word problems. They require you to apply math skills to everyday situations. The hardest thing about doing word problems is translating them into math. The actual problem is often pretty simple. These questions test your ability to set up an equation based on the information in the word problem. The best way to get comfortable with word problems is to practice solving them as much as possible.

Key points regarding word problems:

- Read the entire problem! Don't try to solve anything until you get a feel for the whole problem.
- List the information that is given in order to organize yourself.
- Label variables with what they stand for.
- Determine exactly what the problem is asking. (What do you need to know?)
- Work out the answer.
- Double-check to make sure the answer makes sense. (Check your answer against the original word problem, not your equation.)

Direct Translation into Math

You will be required to translate a verbal description of a mathematical relationship into math terms. Always read the problem carefully and double-check yourself. For instance:

"Nine less than the total of a number and 2" translates into $(n+2) - 9$, or $n - 7$.

"The ratio of 9 more than x to 3" translates into $\dfrac{x+9}{3}$.

"Sarah has four more dollars than Kevin" translates into $S = K + 4$.

"The average of the weights of three children is 80 pounds" translates into $\dfrac{x+y+z}{3} = 80$.

Certain words indicate mathematical operations. Below is a partial list:

$$\text{Addition} \begin{cases} \text{increased by} \\ \text{more than} \\ \text{combined} \\ \text{together} \\ \text{total of} \\ \text{sum} \\ \text{added to} \end{cases} \qquad \text{Subtraction} \begin{cases} \text{decreased by} \\ \text{minus} \\ \text{less} \\ \text{difference between or of} \\ \text{less than} \\ \text{fewer than} \end{cases}$$

$$\text{Multiplication} \begin{cases} \text{of} \\ \text{times} \\ \text{multiplied by} \\ \text{product of} \\ \text{increased or decreased} \\ \text{by a factor of} \end{cases} \qquad \text{Division} \begin{cases} \text{per} \\ \text{a} \\ \text{out of} \\ \text{ratio of} \\ \text{quotient of} \\ \text{percent (divide by 100)} \end{cases}$$

$$\text{Equals} \begin{cases} \text{is} \\ \text{are} \\ \text{was} \\ \text{were} \\ \text{will be} \\ \text{gives} \\ \text{yields} \\ \text{sold for} \end{cases}$$

"Per" and "a" sometimes mean "divided by," as in "I paid $3.00 *per* gallon" (or "$3.00 *a* gallon").

Example 1: The product of two consecutive negative even integers is 24. Find the numbers.

First evaluate the question. Since the two numbers are negative and nonconsecutive, you know that the two numbers are two apart (for example, – 2 and – 4) and, as a result, the second number is two greater than the first.

So, let's call the first number n and the second number n + 2. The question states that the product of the two numbers is 24. Write the question in math terms using the variables you defined:

$$(n)(n+2) = 24$$

Solve for n.

$$n^2 + 2n = 24$$
$$n^2 + 2n - 24 = 0$$
$$(n - 4)(n + 6) = 0$$
$$n = 4 \text{ and } n = -6$$

Since the question stated that the numbers were negative, you can ignore the 4 and take n = – 6 as the solution. Substituting – 6 into n + 2 gives – 4 as the second number.

Example 2: Gloria's washing machine needs fixing. Since her machine is pretty old, she doesn't want to spend more than $100 for repairs. A service call will cost $35, and the labor will be an additional $20 per hour. What is the maximum number of hours that the repairperson can work and keep the total cost at $100?

Let h = the maximum number of hours the repair can take.
Write out an equation based on the information given:
"$35 plus $20 per hour for h hours equals $100."

$$35 + 20h = 100$$
$$20h = 65$$
$$h = \frac{65}{20} = \frac{13}{4} \text{ or } 3\frac{1}{4} \text{ hours}$$

Word Problem Practice Problems

1) A shipment of 100 CDs was just received at a record store. There is a 4% probability that one of the CDs was damaged during shipment, even though the package may not be cracked. If John buys a CD from this shipment, what are the odds that he is buying a damaged CD?

A) $1/25$
B) $4/100$
C) $96/4$
D) $1/24$

2) Peanuts sell for $3.00 per pound. Cashews sell for $6.00 per pound. How many pounds of cashews should be mixed with 12 pounds of peanuts to obtain a mixture that sells for $4.20 per pound?

   A) 3
   B) 4
   C) 6
   D) 8

Note: Answers may be found on Page 114.

If I Had to Guess: The Art of Estimating and Guessing

So what happens if you get stuck? Sometimes you may understand the problem but can't figure out how to solve it. You may have a general idea of what the answer should or shouldn't be, but you can't quite figure out how to get the correct answer. Here are a few tips to increase your chances of choosing the correct answer.

1) **Eliminate** choices that are blatantly incorrect. By eliminating choices, you increase your odds of selecting the correct answer.

2) **Work backwards**. When you're having trouble setting up an equation or interpreting a word problem, you can often work backwards from the answer choices. Pick one of the answer choices and see if it fits all the requirements set forth in the directions.

3) **Figures can be estimated** just by "eyeballing" them. Although figures are not technically drawn to scale, they represent a best representation of the desired result. You can sometime use this if you're stuck on a geometry question.

4) **Use your best guess**. If you are completely at a loss for an answer, use your best guess. When guessing, you should eliminate as many answer choices as possible and then take an "educated" guess from the remaining choices.

Solutions to Practice Problems

Properties of Numbers (Page 51)
1) A
2) D
3) B
4) B
5) D
6) C
7) C
8) E
9) D
10) C
11) A

Fractions (Page 56)
1) E
2) C
3) D
4) C
5) E
6) C

Operations (Page 65)
1) E
2) B
3) C
4) E
5) C
6) A
7) B
8) A

Manipulating Algebraic Expressions (Page 76)
1) D
2) A
3) D
4) C
5) B
6) E

Ratios, Proportions, and Variation (Page 83)
1) B
2) C
3) E
4) C
5) A
6) D
7) E
8) A

Probability and Statistics (Page 87)
1) B
2) D

Geometry (Page 102)
1) D
2) C
3) C
4) A
5) C

Word Problems (Page 106)
1) A
2) D

Chapter Five: SAT Practice Test

VERBAL SECTION I – Writing
(25 minutes, 35 questions) (Answers can be found on page 143.)

Identify the errors in the sentences below. On your answer sheet, fill in the circle that corresponds with the correct answer.

1. Mrs. Williams loves teaching <u>biology, it</u> is one of her favorite subjects.

   A. biology, it
   B. biology, which is a subject that
   C. biology because it
   D. biology and it
   E. biology due to the fact that it

2. She is a wonderful teacher, and it is an honor <u>to be taught by her</u>.

   A. to be taught by her
   B. being taught by her
   C. to be her student
   D. that she is my teacher
   E. getting to have her as a teacher

3. Taking a shot from center <u>ice, the puck that I hit flew</u> straight into the net.

   A. ice, the puck that I hit flew
   B. ice resulted in the puck flying
   C. ice and the puck I hit flew
   D. ice, I hit the puck
   E. ice, the puck was hit

4. Although it's unusually cool for this time of <u>year and a great day to be</u> outside.

   A. year and a great day to be
   B. year, it's a great day for being
   C. year, regardless, it's a great day to be
   D. year, it's a great day to be
   E. year and is a great day for being

5. <u>It is my sincere hope</u> that you will consider joining Key Club.

   A. It is my sincere hope
   B. I sincerely hope
   C. What I sincerely hope is
   D. I am sincerely hoping
   E. The thing that I hope sincerely is

6. After you answer the last question on the test, you should return to <u>what questions, if any, that you</u> skipped.

   A. what questions, if any, that you
   B. whatever questions you
   C. the questions if any are
   D. any questions that you
   E. all those questions that you may have

7. Although most of us have not traveled to exotic lands, <u>there is a natural desire to do this</u>.

   A. there is a natural desire to do this
   B. we naturally desire to do so
   C. our wanting to do it is natural
   D. the desire for us to do so is natural
   E. naturally there is a desire to

8. Contrary to what my grandmother believes, <u>you cannot get sick from breathing cold air.</u>

   A. you cannot get sick from breathing cold air
   B. one cannot get sick just because they breathe cold air
   C. breathing cold air does not result in making you sick
   D. cold air cannot make you sick if you breathe it
   E. cold air cannot cause sickness by being breathed

9. When I went away to <u>college and I finally had to learn</u> how to manage my time.

   A. college and I finally had to learn
   B. college, I finally had to learn
   C. college was when I finally learned
   D. college, that's when I finally learned
   E. college, it was time for me to finally learn

10. Joey's friend Trevor enjoys <u>playing the guitar, listening to music, and milkshakes</u>.

   A. playing the guitar, listening to music, and milkshakes
   B. playing the guitar and listening to music in addition to milkshakes
   C. playing the guitar, he also likes to listen to music and drink milkshakes
   D. guitar, music, and drinking milkshakes
   E. playing the guitar, listening to music, and drinking milkshakes

11. Before we can leave for our hike, <u>our lunches must be packed and our canteens filled with water</u>.

   A. our lunches must be packed and our canteens filled with water
   B. it is necessary for us to pack our lunches and to fill our canteens with water
   C. we must pack our lunches and fill our canteens with water
   D. our lunches must be packed; we must also fill our canteens with water
   E. we must pack our lunches, in addition, we must fill our canteens with water

Identifying Errors

Directions: Identify the errors in the sentences below. On your answer sheet, fill in the circle that corresponds to the error in each sentence.

12. Neither <u>of the ideas</u> <u>you have suggested</u> <u>are feasible</u>, but we appreciate <u>your efforts</u>.　<u>no error</u>
              a   b   c   d   e

13. Amy <u>currently lives</u> in North Carolina, but <u>she spent</u> <u>the majority</u> of her life <u>in central Florida</u>.
            a   b   c   d
   <u>no error</u>
       e

14. <u>To be sure</u> everything <u>runs smoothly</u>, the manager schedules regular meetings <u>that</u> all
        a   b   c
   employees <u>had to attend</u>. <u>no error</u>
                  d   e

15. Someone <u>who attended</u> the <u>benefit dinner</u> left <u>their glasses</u> at the <u>registration desk</u>. <u>no error</u>
                 a   b   c   d   e

16. I enjoyed <u>that movie</u> <u>more than</u> <u>any movie</u> I <u>have seen</u> this year. <u>no error</u>
                   a   b   c   d   e

17. Do you <u>think Jessica</u> <u>will invite</u> <u>you and me</u> to her <u>sixteenth birthday party</u>? <u>no error</u>
                 a   b   c   d   e

18. <u>Whom</u> do <u>you think</u> will win <u>this weekend's</u> big game <u>against the Tigers</u>? <u>no error</u>
       a   b   c   d   e

19. I <u>have been walking</u> <u>all day</u>; I <u>can't wait</u> <u>to set down</u> and relax for a few minutes. <u>no error</u>
              a   b   c   d   e

20. <u>After reading</u> both books, <u>I must say</u> that I like the first one <u>more then</u> <u>the second one</u>. <u>no error</u>
       a   b   c   d   e

21. Let's go <u>out for</u> lunch <u>today; we</u> <u>don't</u> hardly ever <u>spend time</u> together. <u>no error</u>
             a   b c   d   e

22. We <u>need</u> to <u>look in</u> the situation <u>more carefully</u> before <u>we make</u> a decision. <u>no error</u>
        a   b   c   d   e

23. The discovery of two theaters <u>built during</u> <u>Shakespeare's time</u> have excited <u>both scholars and archeologists</u>. <u>no error</u>
                                              a   b   c
    d   e

24. Although Maggie and Hannah both <u>hoped</u> <u>to be a finalist</u> in the talent show, neither of them <u>made</u> it <u>past</u> the first round. <u>no error</u>
                                                    a   b
    c   d   e

25. If <u>one</u> <u>wants to be</u> a concert pianist, you <u>must practice</u> for several hours <u>a day</u>. <u>no error</u>
         a   b   c   d   e

26. Last night I <u>babysat</u> for two children, <u>the youngest</u> <u>of which</u> refused <u>to go to sleep</u>. <u>no error</u>
                  a   b   c   d   e

27. Will you call Trisha and <u>find out</u> <u>whether or not</u> <u>she and Brad</u> want to study for the <u>chemistry</u> test? <u>no error</u>
                             a   b   c   d
    e

28. <u>I can't believe</u> <u>you're taking</u> Jack to the concert <u>even though</u> I like the band <u>more than him</u>.
        a   b   c   d
    <u>no error</u>
      e

29. There <u>has been</u> major changes in <u>Cyndi's attitude</u> <u>toward school</u> <u>lately</u>. <u>no change</u>
              a   b   c   d   e

Paragraph Improvement

Directions: Improve the paragraphs below. On your answer sheet, fill in the circle that corresponds to the correct answer.

Questions 30-35 are based on the following passage:

(1) As students face challenges and try to maintain control of their lives, some begin to develop eating disorders. (2) The two most common eating disorders are anorexia and bulimia. (3) About one in every one hundred 16- to 18-year-olds has anorexia nervosa. (4) Bulimia is even more common. (5) Eating disorders are most common in teenage girls, but they also affect teenage boys. (6) People with anorexia starve themselves, avoid high-calorie foods, and exercise constantly. (7) A normal amount of exercise is important for staying healthy. (8) Those with bulimia eat huge amounts of food and later throw it up. (9) Although people with eating disorders will be quick to say that there's nothing wrong with them, it is important that their friends and family do not give in to their denial and that help is sought for them immediately.

30. Omitting which of the following sentences would improve the unity of the paragraph?

   A. Sentence 3
   B. Sentence 5
   C. Sentence 5
   D. Sentence 7
   E. Sentence 9

31. In context, which of the following is the best way to combine sentences 3 and 4?

   A. About one in every one hundred 16- to 18-year-olds has anorexia nervosa, and bulimia is even more common.
   B. About one in every one hundred 16- to 18-year-olds has anorexia nervosa, bulimia is even more common.
   C. About one in every one hundred 16- to 18-year-olds has anorexia nervosa, however, bulimia is even more common.
   D. Bulimia is even more common than anorexia nervosa, which affects about one in every one hundred 16- to 18-year-olds.
   E. Anorexia nervosa, which is not as common as bulimia, affects about one in every one hundred 16- to 18-year-olds.

32. In context, which of the following is the best way to revise the underlined portion of sentence 9?

   A. friends and family must not give in to their denial, instead they must seek help immediately
   B. friends and family must seek help for them immediately rather than give in to their denial
   C. it is important for friends and family not to give in to their denial but to seek help for them immediately instead
   D. their denial must not be given in to, and help must be sought immediately
   E. friends and family must remember that it is important not to give in to their denial; however, help should be sought immediately

33. Which of the following revisions to sentence 8 is needed to make it consistent with the rest of the passage?

   A. Change "throw" to "threw."
   B. Change "you" to "they."
   C. Replace "it" with "the food."
   D. Add "people" after "Those."
   E. Replace "with" to "who have."

34. Which of the following sentences would be the most effective conclusion for this paragraph?

   A. In conclusion, it is important to know about eating disorders.
   B. Thank you for taking the time to learn about eating disorders.
   C. We should learn as much as we can about eating disorders so we can help ourselves and others.
   D. Education, treatment, and support can save the lives of anorexia and bulimia victims.
   E. To conclude, many students develop eating disorders.

35. This paragraph best represents which type of writing?

   A. persuasive
   B. narrative
   C. expository
   D. creative
   E. descriptive

MATH SECTION I

(20 questions, 25 minutes) (Answers can be found on page 146.)

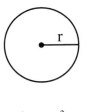 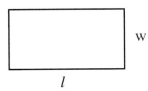 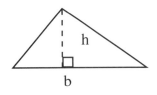 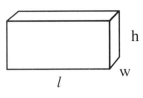

$A = \pi r^2$
$C = 2\pi r$

$A = lw$

$A = \frac{1}{2}bh$

$V = lwh$

 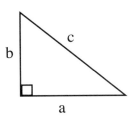 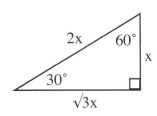 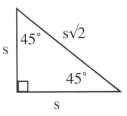

$V = \pi r^2 h$

$c^2 = a^2 + b^2$

Special Right Triangles

The number of degrees in a circle is 360.
The number of degrees in a straight angle is 180.
The sum of the angles of a triangle is 180°.

1) If $3x + 7 = 12$, what is the value of $6x - 5$?

   A) 5
   B) 10
   C) 12
   D) 17
   E) 19

2) There are eight sections of seats in an auditorium. Each section contains at least 300 seats but not more than 400 seats. Which of the following could be the number of seats in the auditorium?

   A) 1600
   B) 2000
   C) 2200
   D) 2600
   E) 3400

3) The points A, B, C, D, and E lie at (−4,0), (−2,0), (2,0), (0,4), and (0,−5) respectively. Which of the following line segments has the greatest length?

   A) $\overline{AD}$
   B) $\overline{BD}$
   C) $\overline{AE}$
   D) $\overline{AC}$
   E) $\overline{CE}$

4) In the figure, MO ⊥ LN, LO = 2, MO = ON, and LM = 4. What is MN?

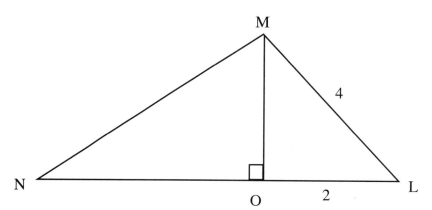

   A) $2\sqrt{6}$
   B) $2\sqrt{3}$
   C) $3\sqrt{2}$
   D) $3\sqrt{3}$
   E) $3\sqrt{3}$

5) The average (arithmetic mean) of x and y is 5, the average of x and z is 8, and the average of y and z is 11. What is the value of z?

   A) 2
   B) 5
   C) 7
   D) 14
   E) 28

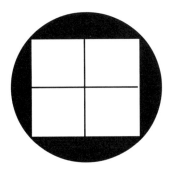

6) In the figure above, each square is tangent to the containing circle at only one point. If the area of each square is x^2, what is area of the shaded region in terms of x?

   A) $(\pi-2)x^2$
   B) $(\pi-4)x^2$
   C) $(4-\pi)x^2$
   D) $(\pi-1)x^2$
   E) $2(\pi-2)x^2$

7) If rstv = 1 and stuv < 0, which of the following must be true?

   A) r > 0
   B) s < 1
   C) t < 0
   D) u ≠ 0
   E) v ≠ 1

8) During a game, the green team scored one-eighth of its points in the first quarter, one-third in the second quarter, one-fourth in the third quarter, and the rmaining points in the fourth quarter. If its total score for the game was 48, how many points did the green team score in the fourth quarter?

   A) 18
   B) 14
   C) 12
   D) 10
   E) 7

9) If $3^{3x} = 81^{x-4}$, what is the value of x?

   A) –4
   B) –2
   C) 4
   D) 12
   E) 16

10) If 7 less than 4 times a certain number is 8 more than the number, what is the number?

   A) –5
   B) –11
   C) 3
   D) 5
   E) 25

11) Find the value of x.

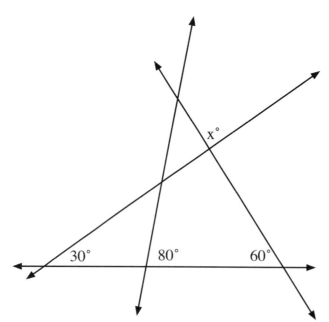

   A) 40°
   B) 50°
   C) 60°
   D) 75°
   E) 90°

x	f(x)
−a	b
a	−b
2a	c

12) The table above shows some of the values for the function f. If f is a linear function, what is the value of the x-intercept in terms of a, b, and c?

A) −2a
B) a−c
C) 2a−b
D) b−c
E) 0

13) 3, 7, −7,...
The first term in the sequence of numbers shown above is 3. Each even numbered term is 4 more than the previous term, and each odd-numbered term after the first is −1 times the previous term. For example, the second term is 3 + 4, and the third term is (−1) x 7. What is the 155th term of the sequence?

A) -7
B) -3
C) 1
D) 3
E) 7

14) In the xy-plane, the equation of line l is $y = -3(x + 2)^2 + 4$. If line m is the reflection of line l in the y-axis, what is the equation of line m?

A) $y=3(x-2)^2 - 4$
B) $y=-3(x-2)^2 + 4$
C) $y=3(x-2)^2 + 4$
D) $y=3(x+2)^2 - 4$
E) $y=3(2-x)^2 + 4$

15) The number x + 8 is how much greater than x − 2?

   A) 6
   B) 10
   C) x − 10
   D) x − 6
   E) x + 6

16) In the figure below, if $\overline{AB}$ = 10, what is the value of k?

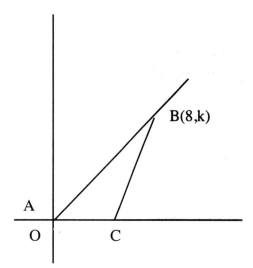

   A) 6
   B) 8
   C) 10
   D) 12
   E) 18

17) If b + 2(x − 4) = s, what is x + 2 in terms of s and b?

   A) $\dfrac{s - b + 12}{2}$
   B) $\dfrac{s - b + 6}{2}$
   C) $\dfrac{12 - s + b}{2}$
   D) $\dfrac{s - b}{2}$
   E) $\dfrac{b - s}{2}$

18) Sarah has at least one quarter, one dime, one nickel, and one penny. If she has three times as many pennies as nickels, the same number of nickels as dimes, and twice as many dimes as quarters, what is the least amount of money she could have?

   A) $0.41
   B) $0.48
   C) $0.58
   D) $0.61
   E) $0.71

19) At a meat processing plant, chickens are accepted only if they weigh between 3.65 and 4.35 pounds. if the plant accepts a chicken weighing m pounds, which of the following describes all possible values of m?

   A) $[m-4] = 0.35$
   B) $[m+4] = 0.35$
   C) $[m-4] < 0.35$
   D) $[m+4] < 0.35$
   E) $[m-4] > 0.35$

20) The set B consists of all even integers between -34 and $2m$. If the sum of these integers is 74, what is the value of m?

   A) 19
   B) 36
   C) 37
   D) 38
   E) 40

VERBAL SECTION II - Critical Reading

(24 questions, 25 minutes) (Answers can be found on page 153.)

Directions: For each question in this section, select the best answer from among the choices given and fill in the corresponding circle on the answer sheet.

1. Some critics suggest that literature leaves us ___, filling our heads with fantasies and distracting us from the ills of society.

    A) benevolent
    B) skeptical
    C) quixotic
    D) prosperous
    E) pragmatic

2. If you're having trouble sleeping, be aware that the use of sleeping pills may be ___, if not downright dangerous.

    A) insufficient
    B) perilous
    C) widespread
    D) beneficial
    E) habitual

3. Now that the company is aware of the buying power of teens, its advertising department is working ___ to ___ the decisions of this market.

    A) cautiously . . . deny
    B) lackadaisically . . . impact
    C) assiduously . . . influence
    D) ardently . . . dissuade
    E) painstakingly . . . pique

4. Because the main course looked so ___, even the least finicky eaters were ___ to try it.

    A) delectable . . . predisposed
    B) appetizing . . . reluctant
    C) unpalatable . . . eager
    D) insipid . . . loath
    E) aberrant . . . intrigued

5. The tiger cubs were not at all ___; in fact, they were as lovable as kittens.

   A) frolicsome
   B) ferocious
   C) affectionate
   D) clamorous
   E) gigantic

6. Although the physics text was ___, the professor's ___ lectures enabled me to pass the course.

   A) ambiguous . . . pellucid
   B) opaque . . . rambling
   C) lucid . . . enigmatic
   D) cryptic . . . equivocal
   E) vague . . . tenebrous

Questions 7-10 are based on the following two reading passages:

(I) One section of our country believes slavery is right, and ought to be extended, while the other believes it is wrong, and ought not to be extended. This is the only substantial dispute. The fugitive-slave clause of the Constitution, and the law for the suppression of the foreign slave trade, are each as well enforced, perhaps, as any law can ever be in a community where the moral sense of the people imperfectly supports the law itself. The great body of the people abide by the dry legal obligation in both cases, and a few break over in each. This, I think, cannot be perfectly cured; and it would be worse in both cases after the separation of the sections, than before. The foreign slave trade, now imperfectly suppressed, would be ultimately revived without restriction, in one section; while fugitive slaves, now only partially surrendered, would not be surrendered at all by the other.

(II) So profoundly ignorant of the nature of slavery are many persons, that they are stubbornly incredulous whenever they read or listen to any recital of the cruelties which are daily inflicted on its victims. They do not deny that the slaves are held as property; but that terrible fact seems to convey to their minds no idea of injustice, exposure to outrage, or savage barbarity. Tell them of cruel scourging, of mutilations and brandings, of scenes of pollution and blood, of the banishment of all light and knowledge, and they affect to be greatly indignant at such enormous exaggerations, such wholesale misstatements, such abominable libels on the character of the southern planters!

7. What is the purpose of the first passage (I)?

   A) to justify the decision of the Confederate states to secede from the Union
   B) to convince readers that separating the nation would only make slavery issues worse
   C) to point out that people around the nation have differing views regarding slavery
   D) to encourage people to obey the laws set forth by the Constitution
   E) to argue about whether slavery is right or wrong

8. What is the purpose of the second passage (II)?

   A) to suggest that people who do not witness slavery first-hand are naive to the severity of the problem
   B) to argue that people with little knowledge about slavery are ignorant
   C) to argue that accounts of the cruelties of slavery are greatly exaggerated
   D) to point out the atrocities of slavery
   E) to voice an opinion about the character of the southern planters

9. According to the author of the first passage, foreign slave trade goes on because

   A) there is no law against it.
   B) citizens haven't yet agreed on whether or not it should be allowed.
   C) fugitive slaves are not fully surrendered.
   D) local slave trade is illegal.
   E) people who don't morally support a law will not enforce it.

10. Based on an examination of both passages, which of the following statements must be true?

    A) The author of the first passage is in favor of slavery.
    B) The author of the second passage is from a northern state.
    C) The second passage is more subjective than the first.
    D) Both passages are intended to put an end to slavery.
    E) Both passages contain primarily objective information.

Questions 11-17 are based on the following passage:

This passage is excerpted from a 1916 American novel. The setting is a small cabin on a mountainside, with no road or other houses visible.

From the little lean-to kitchen the sound of the sputtering suddenly ceased, and at the door appeared a pair of dark, wistful eyes.

"Daddy!" called the owner of the eyes.

There was no answer.

"Father, are you there?" called the voice, more insistently.

From one of the bunks came a slight stir and a murmured word. At the sound the boy at the door leaped softly into the room and hurried to the bunk in the corner. He was a slender lad with short, crisp curls at his ears, and the red of perfect health in his cheeks. His hands, slim, long, and with tapering fingers like a girl's, reached forward eagerly.

"Daddy, come! I've done the bacon all myself, and the potatoes and the coffee, too. Quick, it's all getting cold!"

Slowly, with the aid of the boy's firm hands, the man pulled himself half to a sitting posture. His cheeks, like the boy's, were red--but not with health. His eyes were a little wild, but his voice was low and very tender, like a caress.

"David--it's my little son David!"

"Of course it's David! Who else should it be?" laughed the boy. "Come!" And he tugged at the man's hands.

The man rose then, unsteadily, and by sheer will forced himself to stand upright. The wild look left his eyes, and the flush his cheeks. His face looked suddenly old and haggard. Yet with fairly sure steps he crossed the room and entered the little kitchen.

Half of the bacon was black; the other half was transparent and like tough jelly. The potatoes were soggy, and had the unmistakable taste that comes from a dish that has boiled dry. The coffee was lukewarm and muddy. Even the milk was sour.

David laughed a little ruefully.

"Things aren't so nice as yours, father," he apologized. "I'm afraid I'm nothing but a discord in that orchestra to-day! Somehow, some of the stove was hotter than the rest, and burnt up the bacon in spots; and all the water got out of the potatoes, too,--though that didn't matter, for I just put more cold in. I forgot and left the milk in the sun, and it tastes bad now; but I'm sure next time it'll be better--all of it."

The man smiled, but he shook his head sadly.

"But there ought not to be any 'next time,' David."

"Why not? What do you mean? Aren't you ever going to let me try again, father?" There was real distress in the boy's voice.

The man hesitated. His lips parted with an indrawn breath, as if behind them lay a rush of words. But they closed abruptly, the words still unsaid. Then, very lightly, came these others:--

"Well, son, this isn't a very nice way to treat your supper, is it? Now, if you please, I'll take some of that bacon. I think I feel my appetite coming back."

If the truant appetite "came back," however, it could not have stayed; for the man ate but little. He frowned, too, as he saw how little the boy ate. He sat silent while his son cleared the food and dishes away, and he was still silent when, with the boy, he passed out of the house and walked to the little bench facing the west.

Unless it stormed very hard, David never went to bed without this last look at his "Silver Lake," as he called the little sheet of water far down in the valley.

"Daddy, it's gold to-night--all gold with the sun!" he cried rapturously, as his eyes fell upon his treasure. "Oh, daddy!"

It was a long-drawn cry of ecstasy, and hearing it, the man winced, as with sudden pain.

'Daddy, I'm going to play it--I've got to play it!" cried

the boy, bounding toward the cabin. In a moment he had returned, violin at his chin.

The man watched and listened; and as he watched and listened, his face became a battle-ground whereon pride and fear, hope and despair, joy and sorrow, fought for the mastery.

It was no new thing for David to "play" the sunset. Always, when he was moved, David turned to his violin. Always in its quivering strings he found the means to say that which his tongue could not express.

Across the valley the grays and blues of the mountains had become all purples now. Above, the sky in one vast flame of crimson and gold, was a molten sea on which floated rose-pink cloud-boats. Below, the valley with its lake and river picked out in rose and gold against the shadowy greens of field and forest, seemed like some enchanted fairyland of loveliness. And all this was in David's violin, and all this, too, was on David's uplifted, rapturous face.

11. The author of this passage calls the boy's eyes "wistful" (Paragraph 1/line 3) because he

   A) is wishfully yearning.
   B) is terribly afraid.
   C) is straining to see in the dark.
   D) has been crying.
   E) has poor vision.

12. Which of the following does not provide evidence that the father is in poor health?

   A) His son awakens him for supper.
   B) He winces with pain when his son cries out joyfully.
   C) His cheeks are red, and his eyes are a little wild.
   D) He silently looks at the lake with his son.
   E) He enters the kitchen with fairly sure steps.

13. Based on its use in the passage, the word "ruefully" (Paragraph 12) means

    A) sorrowfully.
    B) quietly.
    C) uncomfortably.
    D) excitedly.
    E) relieved.

14. The father's comment "I think I feel my appetite coming back" (Paragraph 18/line 3) serves to

    A) show that the father is now hungry.
    B) demonstrate the father's desire to protect his son's feelings.
    C) illustrate the father's inconsistent personality.
    D) show that the father's health is improving.
    E) suggest that the food tastes better than he expected.

15. Which of the following does the author use as a metaphor to illustrate the father's internal conflict?

    A) His face looked suddenly old and haggard.
    B) I'm nothing but a discord in that orchestra to-day!
    C) his voice was low and very tender, like a caress
    D) his face became a battle ground
    E) the sky in one vast flame of crimson and gold, was a molten sea

16. Which of the following words best characterizes David?

    A) sullen
    B) defeated
    C) talented
    D) spoiled
    E) innocent

17. The mood of the passage can best be described as

    A) cheerful.
    B) foreboding.
    C) indignant.
    D) regretful.
    E) frustrated.

Questions 18-24 are based on the following passage:

In this passage, an American from the early 1800s writes about his early experiences traveling abroad.

But Europe held forth the charms of storied and poetical association. There were to be seen the masterpieces of art, the refinements of highly-cultivated society, the quaint peculiarities of ancient and local custom. My native country was full of youthful promise: Europe was rich in the accumulated treasures of age. Her very ruins told the history of times gone by, and every mouldering stone was a chronicle. I longed to wander over the scenes of renowned achievement--to tread, as it were, in the footsteps of antiquity--to loiter about the ruined castle--to meditate on the falling tower--to escape, in short, from the commonplace realities of the present, and lose myself among the shadowy grandeurs of the past.

I had, beside all this, an earnest desire to see the great men of the earth. We have, it is true, our great men in America: not a city but has an ample share of them. I have mingled among them in my time, and been almost withered by the shade into which they cast me; for there is nothing so baleful to a small man as the shade of a great one, particularly the great man of a city. But I was anxious to see the great men of Europe; for I had read in the works of various philosophers, that all animals degenerated in America, and man among the number. A great man of Europe, thought I, must therefore be as superior to a great man of America, as a peak of the Alps to a highland of the Hudson; and in this idea I was confirmed, by observing the comparative importance and swelling magnitude of many English travellers among us, who, I was assured, were very little people in their own country. I will visit this land of wonders, thought I, and see the gigantic race from which I am degenerated.

It has been either my good or evil lot to have my roving passion gratified. I have wandered through different countries, and witnessed many of the shifting scenes of life. I cannot say that I have studied them with the eye of a philosopher; but rather with the sauntering gaze with which humble lovers of the picturesque stroll from the window of one print-shop to another; caught sometimes by the delineations of beauty, sometimes by the distortions of caricature, and sometimes by the loveliness of landscape. As it is the fashion for modern tourists to travel pencil in hand, and bring home their portfolios filled with sketches, I am disposed to get up a few for the entertainment of my friends. When, however, I look over the hints and memorandums I have taken down for the purpose, my heart almost fails me at finding how my idle humor has led me aside from the great objects studied by every regular traveler who would make a book. I fear I shall give equal disappointment with an unlucky landscape painter, who had traveled on the continent, but, following the bent of his vagrant inclination, had sketched in nooks, and corners, and by-places. His sketchbook was accordingly crowded with cottages, and landscapes, and obscure ruins; but he had neglected to paint St. Peter's, or the Coliseum; the cascade of Terni, or the Bay of Naples; and had not a single glacier or volcano in his whole collection.

18. The author's desire to go to Europe is based on

    A) idealism kindled by the many books he has read.
    B) his desire to prove that Americans are not inferior to Europeans.
    C) his desire to elevate his position in society.
    D) skepticism promoted by his life in America.
    E) curiosity stemming from previous trips abroad.

19. The word "baleful" (Paragraph 2/line 5) as it is used in this passage means

    A) refreshing.
    B) beneficial.
    C) miserable.
    D) evil.
    E) understandable.

20. Which of the following is not an example of a poetic device used by the author of the excerpt?

    A) every mouldering stone was a chronicle
    B) ruins told the history of times gone by
    C) great man of Europe . . . must therefore be as superior to a great man of America, as a peak of the Alps to a highland of the Hudson
    D) have studied them with the eye of a philosopher
    E) sometimes by the loveliness of landscape

21. The author states that he "...observes the comparative importance and swelling magnitude of many English travelers among us, who, I was assured, were very little people in their own country...." This comment serves to demonstrate

    A) the arrogance of the English.
    B) the greatness of other men in Europe.
    C) the author's lack of confidence.
    D) the scarcity of great men in America.
    E) the insignificance of most Englishmen.

22. In the last paragraph, the author claims that his opportunity to travel has been a "good or evil lot" because

    A) bad things happened during his travels.
    B) he has come to question the world's perceptions of greatness.
    C) he failed to visit the most important sights in Europe.
    D) he liked some aspects of his trip and detested others.
    E) he has mixed feelings about whether or not he wants to return.

23. The author compares himself to a landscape painter who doesn't paint the great landmarks because

    A) he enjoys painting.
    B) he has no artistic ability.
    C) there are no great landscapes left to be painted.
    D) he feels he has wasted his time and failed to see what he went to see.
    E) he prefers to write about the simpler pleasures of the countries he has visited.

24. An important lesson that the author has yet to learn is that

    A) Europe isn't as great as it seems.
    B) you never get a second chance to do the right thing.
    C) greatness is in the eye of the beholder.
    D) no one wants to read stories about print-shops in small towns.
    E) he would have been better off staying at home.

MATH SECTION II

(18 questions, 25 minutes) (Answers can be found on page 156.)

 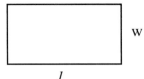 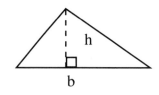 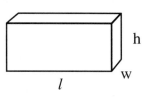

$A = \pi r^2$ $\qquad\qquad A = lw \qquad\qquad A = \frac{1}{2} bh \qquad\qquad V = lwh$
$C = 2\pi r$

 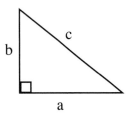 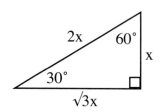 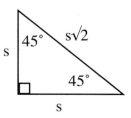

$V = \pi r^2 h \qquad\qquad c^2 = a^2 + b^2 \qquad\qquad$ *Special Right Triangles*

The number of degrees in a circle is 360.
The number of degrees in a straight angle is 180.
The sum of the angles of a triangle is 180°.

1) If $x + \dfrac{2}{x} = \dfrac{11}{3}$, then x can equal which of the following?

   A) $\frac{1}{3}$
   B) 3
   C) $\frac{3}{2}$
   D) 9
   E) 1

2) If $s^2 = 19$, what is the value of $(s + 1)(s - 1)$?

   A) $\sqrt{19} - 1$
   B) $\sqrt{19} + 1$
   C) 18
   D) 20
   E) 35

"All numbers that are divisible by both 2 and 7 are divisible by 3."

2) Which of the following numbers can be used to show that the statement above is FALSE?

   A) 6
   B) 8
   C) 14
   D) 21
   E) 42

4) If the average of a and b is 20 and the average of a, b, and c is 25, what is the value of c?

   A) -15
   B) 10
   C) 15
   D) 25
   E) 35

5) Which of the following represents the values of x that are solutions to the inequality $[3x - 4] > 0$?

   A) $-4/3 < x < 4/3$
   B) $x < 4/3$ or $x > 4/3$
   C) $x > 4/3$
   D) $x > -4/3$
   E) all real numbers

5) Which of the following tables shows a relationship in which z is inversely proportional to x?

A)

z	x
0	2
-2	3
-4	4

B)

z	x
2	4
4	8
6	12

C)

z	x
30	6
15	10
10	16

D)

z	x
40	3
30	4
24	5

E)

z	x
2	6
1	8
0	10

7) Dwayne has a woodshop from which he builds and sells birdhouses. He sells each birdhouse for k dollars. Out of this, one-third is used to pay for the lumber and supplies, and he saves the rest of the money. In terms of k, how many birdhouses must Dwayne sell to save $5000?

A) $15000/k$
B) $k/15000$
C) $k/7500$
D) $7500/k$
E) $7500k$

8) If $x \neq 1$, then $\dfrac{x^2 - 2x + 1}{1} - x = ?$

A) $x - 1$
B) $1 - x$
C) -1
D) $x + 1$
E) $-x - 1$

Student-Produced Response Questions
Fill in your responses on the grids following each question or use the blanks on your answer sheet on page 173. (You may show your work in the space next to the grid.)

9) If $7y - 3x = 24$ and $x = y - 2$, what is the value of y?

10) A construction company built 400 houses last year. Because of rapid growth in the area, the construction of new homes increased 30 percent this year. How many houses did the company build this year?

11) If the ratio of $3x$ to $5y$ is $1/15$, what is the ratio of x to y?

12) The sum of 12 consecutive integers is 5,250. What is the value of the greatest of these integers?

13) What number increased by 3 is equal to 3 less than twice the number?

14) A triangle has base 9, and the other two sides are equal. If the side lengths are integers, what is the shortest possible side?

15) If L is parallel to M, what is the value of y?

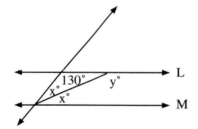

16) In the figure below, $\overline{DA}$ bisects $\angle BAC$, and $\overline{DC}$ bisects $\angle BCA$. If $\angle ADC = 120°$, what is the measure of $\angle B$?

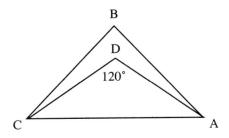

Note: Figure is not drawn to scale.

17) If the area of the square in the figure below is 81 and the perimeter of each of the four triangles is 30, what is the perimeter of the figure outlined by the solid line?

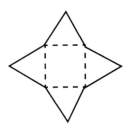

18) A bag contains only white and red marbles. The probability of selecting a red marble is $1/4$. The bag contains 200 marbles. If 50 white marbles are added to the bag, what is the probability of selecting a white marble?

MATH SECTION III
(16 questions, 25 minutes) (Answers can be found on page 161.)

 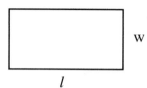 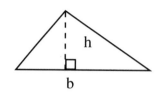 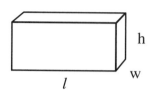

$A = \pi r^2$ $\qquad$ $A = lw$ $\qquad$ $A = \frac{1}{2}bh$ $\qquad$ $V = lwh$
$C = 2\pi r$

 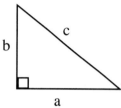 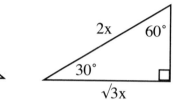 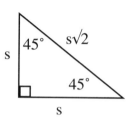

$V = \pi r^2 h$ $\qquad$ $c^2 = a^2 + b^2$ $\qquad\qquad$ *Special Right Triangles*

The number of degrees in a circle is 360.
The number of degrees in a straight angle is 180.
The sum of the angles of a triangle is 180°.

1) For all integers n:

   $\boxed{n} = n^2$ if n is odd
   $\boxed{n} = \sqrt{n}$ if n is even

   What is the value of $\boxed{16} + \boxed{9}$?

   A) 7
   B) 25
   C) 85
   D) 97
   E) 337

2) Over 12 games, a baseball team scored an average of 6 runs per game. If their average number of runs in the first 10 games was 5 and they scored the same number of runs in each of the last two games, how many runs did they score in the last game?

A) 6
B) 11
C) 13
D) 14
E) 17

3) In the figure below, line L is parallel to line M, with angles a, b, c, d, e, f, g, and h as shown. Which of the following lists includes all of the angles that are supplementary to ∠a?

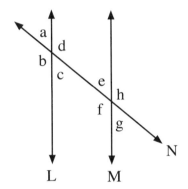

A) b, c, and d
B) b, d, f, and h
C) c, e, and g
D) d, c, g, and h
E) e, f, g, and h

4) In the parallelogram ABCD, BD = 6 and AD = 10. What is the area of ABCD?

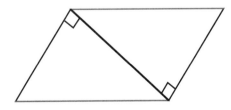

A) 24
B) 30
C) 48
D) 60
E) Cannot be determined from the information given.

5) If $16^{x^2-1} = 64x$, what is a possible value of x?

   A) $1/2$
   B) $-2/3$
   C) $3/2$
   D) $-3/2$
   E) $-1/2$

6) Three nonzero numbers are represented by $6x^2, 5x^2,$ and $10x^2$. What is the ratio of their sum to their product?

   A) $7/100$
   B) $7x^4/100$
   C) $7/100x^3$
   D) $7/100x^4$
   E) $7/100x^6$

7) If $af = 6, fg = 1, ag = 24$ and $a > 0$, find afg.

   A) 4
   B) 6
   C) 8
   D) 12
   E) 144

8) Given the graphs below of f(x) and its transformation, find an expression for the transformation in terms of f(x).

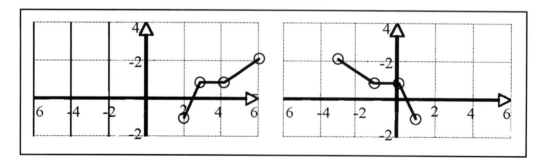

   A) f(x + 3)
   B) f(x − 3)
   C) f(−x − 3)
   D) f(−x +3)
   E) f(−x) +3

9) If the perimeter of the rectangle ABCD is equal to p, and $x = \frac{1}{5}y$, what is the value of y in terms of p?

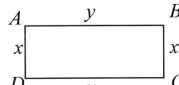

A) $p/3$
B) $5p/12$
C) $5p/8$
D) $5p/6$
E) $p/12$

10) A 12-ton mixture consists of $\frac{1}{6}$ sand, $\frac{2}{6}$ gravel, and $\frac{3}{6}$ cement. If x tons of cement are added, the mixture will contain 60% cement. How many tons of cement need to be added?

A) 1.2
B) 3
C) 3.2
D) 4
E) 5.2

11) The center of a circle is M (0,2), and the endpoint of one of its radii is A (–6,–4). If $\overline{AB}$ is a diameter, what are the coordinates of B?

A) (8,6)
B) (6,8)
C) (4,6)
D) (6,4)
E) (8,10)

12) What is the slope of a line perpendicular to the line represented by the equation $2x – 8y = 16$?

A) – 4
B) – 2
C) – 14
D) 14
E) 4

13) Twice the larger of two numbers is three more than five times the smaller, and the sum of four times the larger and three times the smaller is 71. What is the larger number?

   A) 5
   B) 7
   C) 9
   D) 14
   E) 17

14) The table below gives values of the quadratic function h for selected values of x. Which of the following defines h?

x	0	1	2	3
h(x)	1	2	5	10

   A) $h(x) = x^2 + 1$
   B) $h(x) = x^2 + 2$
   C) $h(x) = 2x^2 - 2$
   D) $h(x) = 2x^2 - 1$
   E) $h(x) = 2x^2 + 1$

15) In the figure below with point A as its center, AB = 10 and AC = $4\sqrt{2}$. What is the area of the shaded region?

   A) $100\pi + 32$
   B) $64\pi + 128$
   C) $36\pi + 128$
   D) $100\pi + 128$
   E) $36\pi + 32$

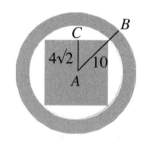

16) What is the surface area of the rectangular prism below?

   A) 312
   B) 336
   C) 360
   D) 384
   E) 432

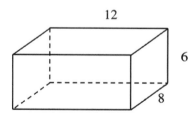

Chapter Six: Answers to Practice Test
(with explanations and solutions)

Verbal Section I – Writing (Test on pages 109-114.)

1. C.
The original sentence is a comma splice (two complete sentences stuck together with a comma). Choices B and E are unnecessarily wordy. Choice D, while not wordy, is a compound sentence and therefore requires a comma before *and*.

2. C.
Choice C changes the voice from passive to active and is brief. Choices A and B are passive voice, and choice D is awkward. Choice E is unnecessarily wordy.

3. D.
The participial phrase ("Taking a shot from center ice") must modify the noun or pronoun closest to it. Since the puck did not take the shot, choices A and E won't work. Choice C changes the sentence to a fragment, and choice B is awkward. Choice D moves *I* to the subject slot; it is also clear and concise.

4. D.
The original sentence is a fragment, as is choice E. Although choices B and C are structurally sound, choice D is a better choice because it's clearer and more concise. (Seeing a pattern yet??)

5. B.
The sentence is clear and concise.

6. D.
Choices A and B inappropriately use *what* and *whatever* as adjectives. Choice C changes the voice to passive, and choice E is wordy.

7. B.
Choices A and E state that there *is* a desire, but not that it is our desire! Choices C and D are the wordy and awkward distractors.

8. A.
Sadly, some teachers say not to use *you* in your writing. However, used correctly, *you* is perfectly acceptable. In choice B, there is disagreement between pronoun (plural *they*) and antecedent (singular *one*). Choice E contains a passive voice verb, and choices C and D are your usual wordy options.

9. B.
Choice A is a sentence fragment. Choices C and D are awkward because of the repetition of *when* in the sentences. Choice E is just wordy.

10. E.
This question is all about parallel structure. Choices A, B, and D are all unparallel. Choice C, while parallel, turns the sentence into a comma splice.

11. C.
Choices A and D both contain passive voice verbs. Choice E makes the sentence a comma splice. Choices B and C are essentially the same, but choice C is more concise and hence the better choice.

12. C.
Subject/verb agreement: The singular subject *neither* requires the verb *is* rather than *are*. Don't be fooled when the test writers put lots of extra words (especially plural words) between the subject and the verb.

13. B.
Verb tense: If she spent most of her life in Florida, we can assume her life is over. However, since we know she currently lives in North Carolina, we must change *spent* to *has spent*.

14. D.
Shift in verb tense: *Runs* and *schedules* are present tense verbs, but *had* is past. Therefore, *had* should be *have*.

15. C. Pronoun/antecedent agreement: *Someone* is singular, so the plural pronoun *their* must be changed to *his* (or *her*).

16. C.
Use of modifiers: We're comparing *that movie* and *any other* movie I have seen. We can't compare *that movie* and *any movie* I have seen because *that movie* is among the movies I have seen.

17. E.
Don't be tricked by choice C. *Me* (an objective pronoun) is correct because it's acting as the direct object.

18. A.
Pronoun case: *Whom* is an objective pronoun and should be changed to *who*, a nominative pronoun, because it's acting as the subject of the clause beginning with *who will win*.

19. D.
Word usage: *Set* should be *sit* because there is no direct object. *Down* tells where (an adverb question) rather than what (a direct object question).

20. C.
Word usage: Use *than* for comparison and *then* for time sequence.

21. C.
Double negative: *Don't hardly* is a double negative. *Don't* can be removed altogether.

22. B.
Idiom: The correct expression is *look into*, not *look in*.

23. C.
Subject/verb agreement: The singular subject *discovery* requires the verb *has* rather than *have*. Again, watch out for subjects and verbs that are separated by lots of other words.

24. B.
Number agreement: Maggie and Hannah can't be *one* finalist; rather, they hoped to be *finalists*.

25. A.
Pronoun case: Notice the shift in pronoun case from *one* to *you*. To be correct, *one* must be changed to *you*. Note that you could also change *you* to *he* or *she*, but *you* is not underlined.

26. B.
Use of modifiers: Use the comparative form (*younger*) to compare two things (*children* in this case). Use the superlative form (*youngest*) only if comparing three or more things.

27. E.
Don't be tricked by choice C. *She* is the correct pronoun because it's acting as part of the subject of *want*. Did you think chemistry should be capitalized? School subjects are capitalized only when they're languages (English, Spanish) or when they're followed by numbers (Algebra I).

28. D.
Pronoun use: This sentence represents incomplete structure. We're really saying, "I like the band more than *he does*." Therefore, we must use *he* rather than *him*.

29. A.
Subject/verb agreement: Watch out for sentences that begin with *there*, which is never a subject. The subject of this sentence is *changes*; therefore, the verb must be *have* rather than *has*.

30. D.
Although the statement is true, it doesn't belong in this paragraph, which focuses on abnormal and unhealthy behavior.

31. A.
Several choices seem to be possible, so use the process of elimination. Choices B and C are comma splices, so we can rule those out. Choice E focuses primarily on anorexia by mentioning bulimia only in the subordinate clause. We want to focus on both in this paragraph. Choice D seems like a great choice, but remember that you're to choose the sentence that works best *in context*. Sentence 2 ends with the word *bulimia*, so starting sentence 3 with the same word is a little awkward. We're left with choice A, which is structurally sound and works well in context.

32. B.

Use the process of elimination again. Choice A is a comma splice. Choice D is passive voice. Choices C and E are needlessly wordy. Choice B gets the job done well.

33. B.

The rest of the paragraph is written in third person, so we shouldn't have a second person pronoun (*you*) stuck in the middle.

34. D.

When concluding an informative paragraph such as this one, it is not appropriate to thank your reader, so eliminate choice B. Since the rest of the paragraph is written in third person, we can eliminate choice C with its first person pronouns (*we*). Choices A and E are way too general; in fact, E just repeats the topic sentence. A good conclusion does more than that. Like choice D, it sums up and helps the reader see the significance of the information.

35. C.

Writing that informs, explains, defines, clarifies, or instructs as its primary purpose is called **expository**.

Math Section I (Test on pages 115-121.)

1) A

$3x + 7 = 12$
$3x = 5$
$x = 5/3$
$6(5/3) - 5 = 10 - 5 = 5$
Therefore, the answer is A.

2) D

Let x represent the number of seats in one section
$300 \text{ seats} \leq x \leq 400 \text{ seats}$

Minimum number of total seats = 300 seats × 8 sections = 2400 seats
Maximum number of total seats = 400 seats × 8 sections = 3200 seats
Therefore, $2400 \leq$ total number of seats ≤ 3200.
The only choice that satisfies the inequality is 2600, choice D.

3) C

You must use the distance formula to solve this problem. For all the line segments in the answers, you must find their lengths.

$$d = \sqrt{(x_2 - x_1)^2 + (y_2 - y_1)^2}$$
$$AD = \sqrt{(-4-0)^2 + (0-4)^2} = \sqrt{16+16} = \sqrt{32} = 4\sqrt{2}$$
$$BD = \sqrt{(-2-0)^2 + (0-4)^2} = \sqrt{4+16} = \sqrt{20} = 2\sqrt{5}$$
$$AE = \sqrt{(-4-0)^2 + (0-(-5))^2} = \sqrt{16+25} = \sqrt{41} = \sqrt{41}$$
$$AC = \sqrt{(-4-2)^2 + (0-0)^2} = \sqrt{36+0} = \sqrt{36} = 6$$
$$CE = \sqrt{(2-0)^2 + (0-(-5))^2} = \sqrt{4+25} = \sqrt{29}$$

Thus, AE is the longest segment and the correct answer choice is C.

4) A

First, find OM using the Pythagorean theorem.

$$4^2 = 2^2 + x^2$$
$$16 = 4 + x^2$$
$$12 = x^2$$
$$x = \sqrt{12} = 2\sqrt{3}$$

Since MO = ON, ON = $2\sqrt{3}$.

Find MN using the Pythagorean theorem.

$$MN^2 = (2\sqrt{3})^2 + (2\sqrt{3})^2$$
$$MN^2 = 12 + 12 = 24$$
$$MN = \sqrt{24} = 2\sqrt{6}$$

5) D

$$\frac{x+y}{2} = 5 \quad \frac{x+z}{2} = 8 \quad \frac{y+z}{2} = 11$$

$x + y = 10 \quad x + z = 16 \quad y + z = 22$
Solve for x, then substitute this expression in the next equation.

$x = 10 - y$
$(10 - y) + z = 16$
$z = y + 6$
Substitute this value in the final equation.

147

$y + y + 6 = 22$
$2y + 6 = 22$
$2y = 16$
$y = 8$
If $y = 8$, then $8 + z = 22$. Thus, $z = 14$, choice D.

6) E

Area of shaded region = area of circle – area of big square
Area of individual square = x^2
Side of individual square = x

First, find the value of the diagonal in one of the small squares, as this is the radius of the circle.

$$x^2 + x^2 = r^2$$
$$2x^2 = r^2$$
Area of circle = $\pi r^2 = 2x^2\pi$
Area of big square = $4x^2$ (4 small squares each with area x^2)
Area of shaded region = $2x^2\pi - 4x^2 = 2x^2(\pi - 2)$

The correct choice is E.

7) D

The only thing absolutely known about these two relationships is that they do not equal zero. Therefore, r, s, t, u, and v $\neq$ 0. The correct choice is D.

8) B

Points in 1st quarter: $1/8$ of 48 = 6
Points in 2nd quarter: $1/3$ of 48 = 16
Points in 3rd quarter: $1/4$ of 48 = 12
Points in first 3 quarters = 6 + 16 + 12 = 34
Points in 4th quarter = total points – points in 1st three quarters = 48 – 34 = 14

9) E

$$3^{3x} = 81^{x-4}$$

Since $81 = 3^4$, the equation becomes: $3^{3x} = (3^4)^{x-4}$

$$3^{3x} = 3^{4x-16}$$
$$3x = 4x - 16$$
$$x = 16$$

10) D

Let "7 less than 4 times a number" = $4x - 7$.

Let "8 more than the number" = $x + 8$.

Set the two equal and solve for x.

$$4x - 7 = x + 8$$
$$3x = 15$$
$$x = 5$$

11) E

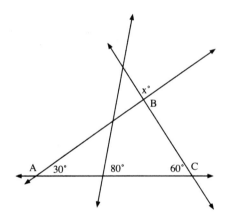

Two angles of triangle ABC sum to 90°, meaning the remaining angle is 90°. By definition of intersecting lines, x = 90°.

12) E

Since $f(a) = -b$ and $f(-a) = b$, the graph of the function passes through the origin (0,0), which happens to be the midpoint between the points (a, –b) and (–a, b). Thus, the x-intercept is the value where $f(x) = 0$. That value is $x = 0$, since it satisfies the function.

13) A

Write out the 1st five terms:

1st term: 3

2nd term: 7

3rd term: −7

4th term: −3

5th term: 3

You are at the beginning of a loop where after every four terms, the 5th term gives the 1st term. To figure out any term:

$$\frac{n^{th}\text{term}}{4}$$

where the remainder will determine which of the initial four values the term will take. For n = 155, $^{155}/_4 = 38^3/_4$ where $^3/_4$ represents that the loop has completed three of the four terms, or equals the 3rd term, − 7.

14) B

Definition for the reflection about the y-axis: for all points, $(x, f(x))$, the reflected graph will contain points $(-x, f(x))$. Thus, a reflection about the y-axis is equivalent to a translation of a point by 2x units, where the line y = 0 is the bisector of the distance between the original position and the new position.

Thus, in the original graph, the vertex is at y = 4 and the graph is shifted right 2 units. In the reflected graph, the vertex occurs at y = 4 but the graph is shifted left 2 units to give the equation: $y = -3(x - 2)^2 + 4$, which is choice B.

15) B

To determine the difference, subtract x − 2 from x + 8.
x + 8 − (x − 2) = x + 8 − x + 2 = 10.

16) A

If you drop a perpendicular down from point B to the x-axis, you will form a right triangle whose hypotenuse is 10 and whose base is 8. To find k, which is the length of the last leg, you will need the Pythagorean theorem.

$$10^2 = 8^2 + k^2$$
$$100 = 64 + k^2$$
$$k^2 = 36$$
$$k = 6$$

17) A

$b + 2(x - 4) = s$

Solve for x.
$$b + 2x - 8 = s$$
$$2x = s - b + 8$$
$$x = \frac{s - b + 8}{2}$$
$$x + 2 = \frac{s - b + 8}{2} + 2 = \frac{s - b + 8}{2} + \frac{4}{2} = \frac{s - b + 12}{2}$$

18) D

Let Q = 2D
   D = N
   N = 3P
where Q = # of quarters, D = # of dimes, N = # of nickels, and P = # of pennies.

If Sarah has one quarter, then she has 2 dimes, 2 nickels, and 6 pennies.

$$1\,Q = \$0.25$$
$$2\,D = \$0.20$$
$$2\,N = \$0.10$$
$$6\,P = \$0.06$$

Total of the least amount of money Sarah can have: $0.61.

19) C

$$\text{Let } m = \# \text{ of pounds}$$
$$3.65 < m < 4.35$$

Because this is an inequality, you can eliminate choices A and B. Go to the remaining answer choices and solve the inequalities.

$$[m - 4] < 0.35$$

Split into two inequalities and solve.
$$m - 4 < 0.35 \text{ and } m - 4 > -0.35$$
$$m < 4.35 \text{ and } m > 3.65 \text{ or } 3.65 < m < 4.35$$

20) A

For the sum to add up to +74, you have to move from − 34 in the positive direction. Thus, the sum of all the negative even integers will be negative. You must have the same values on the positive end to cancel out the negative values. Thus, for a − 34 there must be a + 34. As a result, from − 34 to + 34, the sum is zero. The next two even positive integers are 36 and 38, whose sum is 74.

$$\text{Therefore, } 2m = 38$$
$$m = 19$$

Verbal Section II - Critical Reading (Test on pages 122-131.)

1. C
In this sentence, we need a word that sums up the portion of the sentence following the comma. *Quixotic*, meaning idealistic without regard to practicality, does just that.

2. E
This sentence warns (*be aware*) readers of two negative effects of sleeping pills: They're dangerous and they're [*blank*]. Choices A, C, and D don't work because they are not negative effects. Choice B means the same thing as dangerous and would therefore be redundant. Only choice E provides another effect of sleeping pills appropriate for a warning.

3. C
On the double-blank questions, remember to eliminate one blank at a time. The company wouldn't work lackadaisically (or lazily), so eliminate B. They wouldn't want to deny or dissuade the market, so eliminate A and D. You can pique someone's interest, but you can't pique a decision, so E doesn't make sense.

4. D
Even the least finicky eaters wouldn't be eager to eat something that looks unpalatable or intrigued to eat something that looks aberrant, so eliminate C and E. Nor would they be reluctant to eat something that looks appetizing, so eliminate B. However, even an eater who is not picky would be hesitant to eat something that looks tasteless, so D is the best choice.

5. B
This sentence calls for a characteristic that is opposite of lovable. Only ferocious fits the bill.

6. A
The word *although* in this sentence tells us we're looking for opposites. If the professor's lectures helped the speaker pass the course, then the lectures were clearer than the text. Hence, A is the only choice that works here.

7. B
Although the author does point out that people have different views (choice C), his main point in the paragraph is to argue that those differences will only be made worse if the nation separates.

8. A
The author does mention the atrocities of slavery but only as an illustration to make his main point about the naivety of people removed from the problem.

9. E
The author states directly that the law is enforced as well as any law can be "in a community where the moral sense of the people imperfectly supports the law itself." In other words, if people don't believe in the spirit of the law, they're not going to work hard at enforcing it.

10. C

There is no question that the second passage contains more subjective information. It is full of opinion and charged language. Although choices A and B may be true, there is no evidence to support them. The purpose of the first passage, as addressed in question 7, is to discourage separation of the nation; therefore, choice D can't be correct. Nor can choice E, since we have already established the fact that the second passage is subjective rather than objective.

11. A

You must read on further to determine how the boy feels here. He has tried so hard to prepare a meal and desperately wants his father to be pleased with it. The passage provides no evidence for the other choices.

12. D

Although the other choices all point to physical or emotional strain, a man need not be unhealthy to look silently at a lake.

13. A

The boy tries to laugh, but he feels sorrow because the entire meal is ruined. Also, he apologizes in the next paragraph. Choice C seems possible, but based on his attitude toward his father up to this point in the passage, we know that he feels comfortable around his father and just wants very much to please him.

14. B

It is necessary to look at the preceding paragraphs to understand the meaning of this line. The father holds back any comments that might hurt the boy's feelings and "lightly" says he's eager to eat some of his supper. The fact that he doesn't eat much confirms that the comment is intended to spare the boy's feelings.

15. D

Choices A and C are not metaphors, so they can be eliminated. Choices B and E, although metaphors, do not refer to any type of struggle on the father's part. Choice D provides an outward sign of his internal struggle. His face is a battle ground as the battle is waged inside him.

16. E

David shows his innocence in many ways throughout the passage, especially in his joy and optimism in spite of the obvious undercurrent of sadness. The father has clearly protected his son from sorrow to the best of his ability.

17. B

Plenty of foreshadowing throughout the passage suggests that something bad will happen. Although the boy is cheerful, the reader realizes that it is only his innocence that allows him to feel this way.

18. A

In the first paragraph of the passage, the author speaks of the grand illusions he has of Europe. In the second paragraph, he mentions philosophical works that have led him to believe in the grandeur of Europe.

19. C

The word baleful is used today to mean evil or sinister, but in the early 1800s it meant miserable as well. A close look at the context clues in the passage should make the meaning clear. Remember, in this section of the test, you will be asked to figure out the meanings of words *as they are used in passages*.

20. D

Although the author uses all of these lines, only choice D does not include a poetic device. Choice A is a metaphor; choice B is personification; choice C is a simile; and choice E is an example of alliteration.

21. B

The author reasons that, if these little men are so important, others in their country must be truly great. Don't be tricked by choice A. As readers, we detect arrogance in the Englishmen he speaks about, but the naive author is sincere, not sarcastic.

22. C

Although it's good that he was able to travel, he's frustrated by the fact that he returned home without seeing what he set out to see.

23. D

Rather than taking in the great sights, he enjoyed the small towns. Once he returned home, however, his heart almost fails him when he realizes that he missed out on the sights of the "regular traveller."

24. C

The things the author saw in his travels may not be considered important by "regular travelers," but that doesn't make them any less great. The author must learn that it's okay to appreciate things that others deem unimportant.

Math Section II (Test on pages 132-137.)

1) B

$$x + \frac{2}{x} = \frac{11}{3}$$

Multiple everything by 3x, then solve the resulting quadratic equation.

$3x \left(x + \frac{2}{x} = \frac{11}{3} \right)$
$3x^2 + 6 = 11x$
$3x^2 - 11x + 6 = 0$
$(3x - 2)(x - 3) = 0$
$x = \frac{2}{3}$ or $x = 3$
Since $x = 3$, the correct choice is B.

2) C

$(s + 1)(s - 1) = s^2 - 1$
Since $s^2 = 19$, $s^2 - 1 = 18$

3) C

All are divisible by 3 except for 8 and 14. 8 is not divisible by 7, so that leaves 14.

4) E

$$\frac{a + b}{2} = 20 \quad \text{and} \quad \frac{a + b + c}{3} = 25$$

$a + b = 40$ and $a + b + c = 75$

Plug in the value of a + b.

$40 + c = 75$
$c = 35$

5) B

Set up the two inequalities and solve:
$$3x - 4 > 0 \text{ and } 3x - 4 < 0$$
$$x > {}^4/_3 \text{ and } x < {}^4/_3$$

6) D

To be inversely proportional, $xz = k$, where k is a constant.
Thus, as x increases, z decreases in proportion to constant k.
Choice D is the only choice that has a consistent k value ($k = 120$).
As z increases, x decreases.

7) D

Of Dwayne's sales, he pays ${}^k/_3$ for lumber and supplies. That leaves ${}^{2k}/_3$ for savings.
To save $5000, Dwayne must sell:
$$\frac{5000}{\frac{2k}{3}} = 5000 \cdot \frac{3}{2k} = \frac{15000}{2k} = \frac{7500}{k}$$

8) B

Factor the numerator:
$$x^2 - 2x + 1 = (x - 1)(x - 1)$$
Examine the denominator:
$$1 - x = -1(x - 1)$$
Solve the expression.
$$\frac{(x - 1)(x - 1)}{-1(x - 1)} = -(x - 1) = 1 - x$$

Solutions to Student-Produced Response Questions

9)   9/2 or 4.5

    Substitute $x = y - 2$ into $7y - 3x = 24$, then solve for y.

$$7y - 3(y - 2) = 24$$
$$7y - 3y + 6 = 24$$
$$4y = 18$$
$$y = {}^{18}\!/_4 = {}^{9}\!/_2$$

10)   520

    Percent increase = 30% or 0.3
    Increased number of houses built = 400 (0.3) = 120 houses
    Total houses built in new year = 400 + 120 = 520 houses.

11)   1/9

    Write ratio as a fraction: ${}^{3x}\!/_{5y} = {}^{1}\!/_{15}$
    Cross multiply: $45x = 5y$
    Setup desired ratio: ${}^{x}\!/_y = {}^{5}\!/_{45} = {}^{1}\!/_9$

12)   443

    This problem involves an arithmetic series, so you need the equation for the sum of an arithmetic series:

$$\text{Sum of arithmetic series} = {}^{n}\!/_2 \, (2a_1 + (n - 1)d)$$

    You are given that the sum = 5250, the number of terms (n) = 12, and d (difference between terms) equals 1. You will need to find the first term, a_1 in order to find the 12th term.

    Plug the given values into the equation and solve for a_1.
$$5250 = {}^{12}\!/_2 \, (2a_1 + (12 - 1)(1))$$
$$5250 = 6(2a_1 + 11)$$
$$875 = 2a_1 + 11$$
$$2a_1 = 864$$
$$a_1 = 432$$

Next you need the equation for the nth term of an arithmetic series:

$$a_n = a_1 + (n-1)d$$

Plug in the values $n = 12$, $d = 1$, and $a_1 = 432$ to find a_{12}.

$$a_{12} = 432 + (12-1)(1) = 432 + 11 = 443.$$

13)   6

Let "what number increased by three" = $x + 3$.
Let "three less than twice the number" = $2x - 3$.

$$x + 3 = 2x - 3$$
$$x = 6$$

14)   5

The triangle inequality rule states that the sum of the lengths of any two sides of a triangle is greater than the length of the third side.

$$\text{Base} = 9$$

Let one of the other sides = x

$$\text{Then } x + x > 9$$
$$2x > 9$$
$$x > 9/2 \text{ or } 4.5$$

Since the sides are integers, the shortest possible side would be ~5.

15)   25

By definition of parallel lines cut by a transversal, $x + y = 180$ and
$$x + x + 130 = 180.$$

Solve for x.
$$2x + 130 = 180$$
$$2x = 50$$
$$x = 25$$

Plug x into the next equation to find y.
$$x + y = 180$$
$$25 + y = 180$$
$$y = 155$$

16) 60

    △CDA is proportionate to △CBA.
    Since DA is a bisector, you know that ∠DAC = ½ ∠BAC.
    The same relationship is true for ∠DCA and ∠BCA (∠DCA = ½ ∠BCA).
    The relationship between ∠B and ∠D should be inversely proportional due to the fact that as D approaches B, ∠D would decrease inversely to the other angles. Thus, ∠B is 60° based on scaling ∠D by ½.

17) 84

    If the area of the square = 81, then each side of the square is 9.
    If the perimeter of each △ = 30, then:

    Perimeter of bold outlined figure = sum of perimeters of all triangles – perimeter of square, since the dashed side of each triangle is a side of the square.

    Since there are four triangles each with a dashed side, that equals the perimeter of the square.

    The perimeter of the square is 9 + 9 + 9 + 9 = 36.
    Thus, 4 (30) – 36 = 120 – 36 = 84

18) 4/5 or 0.8

    Probability (red) = ¼ out of 200 marbles = 50 red marbles
    Initial number of white marbles = 200 – 50 = 150 white marbles
    150 white marbles + 50 white marbles = total of 200 white marbles
    Total number of marbles = 200 white + 50 red = 250 marbles
    Probability of selecting a white marble = $^{200}/_{250}$ = $^{4}/_{5}$

Math Section III (Test on pages 138-142.)

1) **C**

Since ⬜16⬜ is even, you must use the second relationship. Thus, ⬜16⬜ = $\sqrt{16}$ = 4. Since ⬜9⬜ is odd, ⬜9⬜ = 9^2 = 81. 4 + 81 = 85. Thus, the answer choice is C.

2) **B**

Let x = total number of runs
$x/12$ = 6 runs per game for the 12 games
x = 72 total runs
Now set up another relationship for the first 10 games.
Let y = number of runs in the first 10 games
$y/10$ = 5
y = 50 runs in the first 10 games
Number of runs in last the 2 games = (total runs) – (runs in the first 10 games)
= 72 – 50 = 22 runs in the last two games
If the team scored the same number of runs in the last 2 games, then $22/2$ = 11 run per game in each of the last 2 games.

3) **B**

By definition of intersecting lines, ∠a = ∠c; thus, you can eliminate any choice that has ∠c in it (choices A, C, and D. Also, ∠a is supplementary to ∠d and ∠b. Thus, ∠b = ∠d. By definition of parallel lines cut by a transversal, ∠b = ∠h = ∠f.
Thus, b, d, h, and f must all be supplementary to ∠a. The choice is therefore B.

4) C

The easiest way to determine the area is to find the area of one triangle, then double the result (both triangles are equal). To find the area of one of the triangles, you need to find the third side. Using the Pythagorean theorem:

$$a^2 + 6^2 = 10^2$$
$$a^2 + 36 = 100$$
$$a^2 = 64$$
$$a = 8$$

Since $\triangle ABD$ is a right triangle, the base and height are each of the triangle's legs.

Area of one triangle = $\frac{1}{2}(6)(8) = 24$

Area of parallelogram = 2x (area of one triangle) = 2 x 24 = 48. Thus, the answer is C.

5) E

$$16^{x^2} - 1 = 64^x$$
$$(4^2)^{x^2-1} = (4^3)^x$$
$$4^{2x^2-2} = 4^{3x}$$
$$2x^2 - 2 = 3x$$
$$2x^2 - 3x - 2 = 0$$

Factor.

$$(2x + 1)(x - 2) = 0$$
$$x = -\frac{1}{2} \text{ or } x = 2$$

Because $x = -\frac{1}{2}$, the answer is E.

6) D

Sum = $6x^2 + 5x^2 + 10x^2 = 21x^2$

Product = $6x^2 \cdot 5x^2 \cdot 10x^2 = 300x^6$

Ratio of sum to product = $\dfrac{21x^2}{300x^6} = \dfrac{7}{100x^4}$

The answer choice is D.

7) D

Solve for f in $af = 6$.
$$f = 6/a$$
Plug this value for f into $fg = 1$.
$$(6/a)g = 1$$
$$g = a/6$$
Plug this value of g into $ag = 24$.
$$a(a/6) = 24$$
$$a^2/6 = 24$$
$$a^2 = 144$$
$$a = \sqrt{144} = 12$$

Thus,
$$f = 6/12 \text{ or } 1/2 \text{ and } g = 12/6 \text{ or } 2$$
So, $afg = 12 \cdot (1/2) \cdot 2 = 12$, choice D.

8) D

The second graph represents the inverse of the original function $(-x)$ followed by a translation of 3 to the left: $(-x + 3)$. Therefore, the answer is D.

9) B

The perimeter of the rectangle $(p) = 1/5 y + 1/5 y + y + y = 12/5 y$
$p = 12/5 y$
To express y in terms of p, multiply both sides by $5/12$ to give: $y = 5p/12$.
The answer is B.

10) B

For the 12-ton mixture: 6 tons = sand and gravel ($1/6 + 2/6 = 3/6$ or $1/2$ of mixture)
6 tons = cement

Set up the problem in terms of a percentage ratio:

If x = tons of cement added, let x + 12 = total # of tons of mixture.

Let x + 6 = tons cement added + cement in initial mixture.

x + 6 is 60% of x + 12

$$\frac{x+6}{x+12} = \frac{60}{100}$$

100x + 600 = 60x + 720

40x = 120

x = 3

Therefore, the answer is B.

11) B

Use the distance formula to first find the length of the radius.

$$d = \sqrt{(x_2 - x_1)^2 + (y_2 - y_1)^2}$$

$\sqrt{(-6-0)^2 + (-4-2)^2} = \sqrt{36+36} = \sqrt{72} = 6\sqrt{2}$

Then use the formula with the center and each of the answer choices to find which choice has the same length.

When you use this formula with (6,8):

$\sqrt{(6-0)^2 + (8-2)^2} = \sqrt{36+36} = \sqrt{72} = 6\sqrt{2}$

This B is the answer.

12) D

2x − 8y = 16

− 8y = − 2x + 16

y = $1/4$x − 2

Thus, m = $1/4$ and the answer is D.

13)   D

$$\text{Let } x = \text{larger number}$$
$$\text{Let } y = \text{smaller number}$$

The relationships derived from the text are:

$$2x = 5y + 3 \text{ and } 4x + 3y = 71$$

Solve for x in the first equation, then plug that value into the second equation.

$$x = \frac{5y + 3}{2}$$

$$4\left(\frac{5y + 3}{2}\right) + 3y = 71$$

$$10y + 6 + 3y = 71$$
$$13y + 6 = 71$$
$$13y = 65$$
$$y = 5$$

Now plug y = 5 into the first equation and solve for x.

$$2x = 5(5) + 3$$
$$2x = 28$$
$$x = 14$$

14)   A

Start with x = 0. When x = 0, h(x) = 1. Therefore, 1 must be added somewhere in the equation. Look at the choices and eliminate B, C, and D because none of them involves adding 1. Plug x = 1 into the remaining equations to see which one satisfies the table.

$$x^2 + 1 = (1)^2 + 1 = 2 \text{ (satisfies function)}$$
$$2x^2 + 1 = 2(1)^2 + 1 = 3 \text{ (does not satisfy function)}$$

The answer is A.

15) C

The area of the outer circle is 100π.
To find the area of the inner circle, you need to find the length of its radius. The radius of the inner circle is the diagonal of the square.
Use the Pythagorean theorem to find the length of the diagonal. The diagonal of a square forms two 45°- 45°- 90° right triangles, so the legs of the triangle formed with the square will be equal ($4\sqrt{2}$).

$$(4\sqrt{2})^2 + (4\sqrt{2})^2 = c^2$$
$$32 + 32 = c^2$$
$$64 = c^2$$
$$c = 8$$

Thus, the area of the inner circle is 64π.
One side of the square equals $4\sqrt{2} + 4\sqrt{2} = 8\sqrt{2}$
The area of the square is $(8\sqrt{2})^2 = 128$.

area of the shaded region (A) = area of outer circle – area of inner circle + area of square

$$A = (100\pi - 64\pi) + 128 = 36\pi + 128$$

16) E

There are six faces to the prism. Within the six faces, there are three pairs of equal faces.

Area of first face of one pair: 6 x 8 = 48 x 2 faces = 96
Area of first face of second pair: 12 x 8 = 96 x 2 faces = 192
Area of first face of third pair: 6 x 12 = 72 x 2 faces = 144

Total surface area = 96 + 192 + 144 = 432. Thus, the answer is E.

Chapter Seven: Additional Resources

You may find these additional resources helpful as you prepare for the *SAT Reasoning Test* and move toward college planning:

- **Club Z! Tutoring (www.ClubZ.com)**

- ***The Hipp List* by IVY1600, Inc. (www.ivy1600.com)**

- ***Tooth and Nail: A Novel Approach*, by Charles Harrington Elster and Joseph Elliott**

- **The College Board (www.collegeboard.com)**

- **My College Options (www.mycollegeoptions.org)**

- **The National Association for College Admission Counseling (www.nacacnet.org)**

- ***The Road to College: A High School Student's Guide to Discovering Your Passion, Getting Involved, and Getting Admitted*, by Joyce E. Suber and the Staff of The Princeton Review.**

About the Authors

Dawn Burnette, author of the verbal section of *The Essential Guide to the SAT*, is a National Board Certified Teacher who has taught high school English for fifteen years. She is also certified by the State of Georgia in gifted education for grades K-12. Dawn holds a B.A. in English Education and Journalism from Lenoir-Rhyne College and an M.A. in English Education from Georgia State University.

In addition to her work on this guide, Dawn has published several works, including *Daily Grammar Practice* (a program for helping students in first grade through college to understand, remember, and apply grammar concepts); *The Burnette Writing Process* (an individualized, web-supported writing approach for grades 6-12); *Vocabulary: A Novel Solution* (a literature-based vocabulary program); and *DGP Plus: Building Stronger Writers* (writing strategies for helping students transfer grammar concepts to writing).

A finalist for 2007 Georgia Teacher of the Year and recipient of a National Council of Teachers of English Teacher of Excellence Award, Dawn has spoken at conferences and to school systems all around the country.

Stefan France, author of the mathematics section of *The Essential Guide to the SAT* graduated from Duke University in 2000 with a B.S. in Chemistry. Stefan has earned numerous academic awards for his outstanding scholarship and abilities in math and science.

After obtaining his Ph.D. in Chemistry from The Johns Hopkins University in 2005, Stefan joined Emory University as a postdoctoral associate. In 2007, he joined the faculty at Georgia Institute of Technology as an assistant professor of chemistry. He has also served as a math tutor for middle and high school students at ClubZ!.

Terry Wilfong, Terry Wilfong is one of the nation's top experts on financing college and admissions and has worked with hundreds of colleges and universities across the U.S., counseling students in every aspect of college admissions. For over 15 years, Terry has lectured and coached tens of thousands of parents, students and educators at thousands of high schools, churches and special events across the country.

Terry has received numerous awards and recognitions including the McArthur Award for the most outstanding junior officer in the United States Army, the President's Recognition Award for educational marketing and recruitment, and the Communicator Award for Excellence. Terry is also a syndicated columnist, producing weekly and monthly articles on college admissions and financing.

Co-Authors: The Student Perspective

Diane Darling is a recent high school graduate. While still attending high school, she was a full-time student in the University of West Georgia's dual enrollment program, taking college courses while earning her diploma. She maintained a 4.0 GPA and scored in the top 95% of her class on both the SAT and ACT exams.

Erin Gard recently graduated early from high school and enrolled at Georgy State University in Atlanta. Erin scored in the top 98% of her clas on the SAT exam.

Joyce Suber, author and editor of The Essential Guide to the SAT, is a seasoned educator. A graduate of the University of Illinois, she holds a B.A. degree in Sociology and earned a 4.0 in the graduate Educational Psychology program at the National College of Education (National-Louis University). Joyce is certified by the State of Illinois to teach grades K-12, with concentrations in Language Arts and Social Studies (grades 6-12), and has taught high school English in both public and independent schools.

In 2007, Joyce completed a book published by The Princeton Review (Random House) entitled *Road to College: A High School Student's Guide to Discovering Your Passion, Getting Involved, and Getting Admitted*. She has served on numerous boards and committees of professional organizations in the field of college admission counseling. She has also spoken at numerous conferences and schools throughout the United States.

The Essential Guide to the SAT - Practice Test

Name: _____

Verbal Sec. I (test on page 109-114)	**Math Sec. I** (test on page 115-121)
1. A B C D E	1. A B C D E
2. A B C D E	2. A B C D E
3. A B C D E	3. A B C D E
4. A B C D E	4. A B C D E
5. A B C D E	5. A B C D E
6. A B C D E	6. A B C D E
7. A B C D E	7. A B C D E
8. A B C D E	8. A B C D E
9. A B C D E	9. A B C D E
10. A B C D E	10. A B C D E
11. A B C D E	11. A B C D E
12. A B C D E	12. A B C D E
13. A B C D E	13. A B C D E
14. A B C D E	14. A B C D E
15. A B C D E	15. A B C D E
16. A B C D E	16. A B C D E
17. A B C D E	17. A B C D E
18. A B C D E	18. A B C D E
19. A B C D E	19. A B C D E
20. A B C D E	20. A B C D E
21. A B C D E	
22. A B C D E	
23. A B C D E	
24. A B C D E	
25. A B C D E	
26. A B C D E	
27. A B C D E	
28. A B C D E	
29. A B C D E	
30. A B C D E	
31. A B C D E	
32. A B C D E	
33. A B C D E	
34. A B C D E	
35. A B C D E	

The Essential Guide to the SAT - Practice Test

Name: _____

Verbal Sec. II (test on page 122-131)	**Math Sec. II** (test on page 132-137)	**Math Sec. III** (test on page 138-142)
1. A B C D E	1. A B C D E	1. A B C D E
2. A B C D E	2. A B C D E	2. A B C D E
3. A B C D E	3. A B C D E	3. A B C D E
4. A B C D E	4. A B C D E	4. A B C D E
5. A B C D E	5. A B C D E	5. A B C D E
6. A B C D E	6. A B C D E	6. A B C D E
7. A B C D E	7. A B C D E	7. A B C D E
8. A B C D E	8. A B C D E	8. A B C D E
9. A B C D E	9. _____	9. A B C D E
10. A B C D E	10. _____	10. A B C D E
11. A B C D E	11. _____	11. A B C D E
12. A B C D E	12. _____	12. A B C D E
13. A B C D E	13. _____	13. A B C D E
14. A B C D E	14. _____	14. A B C D E
15. A B C D E	15. _____	15. A B C D E
16. A B C D E	16. _____	16. A B C D E
17. A B C D E	17. _____	
18. A B C D E	18. _____	
19. A B C D E		
20. A B C D E		
21. A B C D E		
22. A B C D E		
23. A B C D E		
24. A B C D E		